Mental Illness: Survival and Beyond

Mental Illness: Survival and Beyond

A Practical Guide to the Inpatient Psychiatric Experience

Virginia S. Wilson

Canadian Cataloguing in Publication Data

Wilson, Virginia S. (Virginia Susan), 1953-
  Mental illness

  Includes bibliographical references.
  ISBN 1-55212-213-1

  1. Psychiatric hospital care. 2. Psychiatric
hospital patients. I. Title.
RC439.W54 1998   362.2'1   C98-910873-2

TRAFFORD

This book was published "on-demand" in cooperation with Trafford Publishing.
On-demand publishing is a unique process and service of making a book available for retail
sale to the public taking advantage of on-demand manufacturing and Internet web marketing.
On-demand publishing includes promotions, retail sales, manufacturing, order fulfilment,
accounting and collecting royalties on behalf of the author.

Suite 2, 3050 Nanaimo St., Victoria, B.C. V8T 4Z1, CANADA

Phone	250-383-6864	Toll-free	1-888-232-4444 (Canada & US)
Fax	250-383-6804	E-mail	sales@trafford.com
Web site	www.trafford.com	TRAFFORD PUBLISHING IS A DIVISION OF TRAFFORD HOLDINGS LTD.

Trafford Catalogue #98-0031   www.trafford.com/robots/98-0031.html

10   9   8   7   6   5   4   3   2

For my Father and his lovely wife.

Table of Contents

Acknowledgments

This book was written to thank, in a tangible way, all the many people, both consumers and professionals, who have helped me to be as well as I am today. Of these, Dr. G. Nestadt deserves special mention for his kindness and persistence. I also owe a great debt to Drs. Stanley E. Greben and John K. McComb. They are both generous enthusiastic therapists, and provided unstinting encouragement and advice during the writing and production of this book.

The Hazelton Writers' Group of Toronto gave me cheerful and constructive help with the text, when I know they would rather have been reading something else.

The publication of this book was funded by a bursary from the Ontario Psychiatric Association, and a grant from the Albert and Temmy Latner Foundation, the receipt of which was facilitated by the Canadian Mental Health Association.

I must also thank Mr. Murray Lamb for looking over the text, and Cory Jones and Jeff Meyer for help with the medication tables, Gordon Robertson for advice on cover design, and friends Jane, Murray, Gracie and Emma for their unequivocal support. The people at Trafford also deserve thanks for doing what they do so well.

Lastly I thank my husband Alan for being there, always, and for so much more than just the typesetting.

Introduction

This book is intended to give you practical help if you, your loved one, or your patient is hospitalized for a psychiatric illness. Practical matters, such as the searching of possessions and the allocation of "privileges" are discussed, along with some notes on how the hospitalized person is likely to feel during the various stages of the process. The aim of this is to help the person get the most out of his or her stay, minimize its length, and feel less alone during the process.

The book is structured to accompany you, the consumer, through the process, given the difficulties you may be experiencing at each stage. So the first chapter is presented simply, only because I can remember being so distressed that I could not concentrate enough to read effectively. The later chapters contain more lengthy passages, and are intended to be read only after you have started to feel better. The last chapter is meant for that time after your discharge, when you have to cope alone.

When this book was first written, people usually stayed in the hospital for six to eight weeks. Today, many people are discharged after only a few days. This mystifies me. The new medications available now are very effective, but not so much as to cure someone in less than a week. The brutal fact is that many are discharged prematurely. More and more consumers are having to get by with very little help, and many of them are homeless. In response to this appalling circumstance, I have restructured this book to expand the chapters that discuss ways of managing a mental illness outside the hospital environment.

Although this book is addressed to the consumer, there are others who may find it useful. Psychiatric residents, student nurses, social workers and occupational therapists, could find this volume helps them to relate to their patients. Family members and friends might feel less bewildered after reading it. I hope that the policy-makers might derive some insight from it, but I suspect that this is wishful thinking. If any of these groups increase their understanding of mental illness, then consumers are helped, which is the sole purpose of the book.

Lastly I would like to state that I will refer to people with mental illness as consumers, because this is the term that they prefer.

I have a slight problem with this word, however, because it seems to imply an element of choice. I believe that mental illness is <u>illness</u>, as real and legitimate as any other, and people have no choice about whether or not they will be afflicted by it. I do not object to the term 'survivor' in this context. Recovery from mental illness is a matter of survival, and that is what this book is all about.

· 1 ·
Your Time in the Hospital

In this chapter, important sentences will be placed in bold type, with explanations to follow. Do not bother with the explanations if you do not feel like it. Save them for when you feel better.

The First Day

Someone has brought you to the hospital. They say you are mentally ill. You are shocked and appalled. Here are some things you should know.

> **You will be interviewed. Be as honest as you can. The sooner your pain is understood, the sooner you will be able to leave.**

Whatever the circumstances were that brought you to the hospital, you will be interviewed before you are admitted. You may or may not have seen a psychiatrist before. You may be afraid, angry, or confused, or so disoriented that nothing makes any sense. The only way, however, to get the help you need is to be absolutely honest about how you feel and how things seem to you. Some of the questions will sound fairly stupid, but do your best to answer them. As with any other illness, the doctor cannot help you unless he or she knows what is wrong, and the things you say and do are all he has to work on, at first. A medical student may attend, or even conduct, the interview, but do not let this disturb you — she or he will not be making any major decisions in your treatment.

> **You will be taken to a ward. Expect your things to be searched. They do it to everyone.**

After your interview you will be taken to the psychiatric ward to which you have been assigned. Often, in a busy hospital, the choice of ward will simply be decided on the basis of space.

1

Similarly, your allocation to a particular treatment team is likely to be decided by the time of day that you arrived. These treatment teams usually consist of a psychiatrist, one or more residents, a number of nurses, and a social worker. There may also be an occupational therapist (OT). The system varies from place to place. The procedure will also depend on your condition and the degree of attention you need. One of the nurses will take charge of you and perform the practical aspects of admission.

Your things will be searched. This is not a personal insult but is necessary for the safety of everyone on the ward, yourself included. I have found that most staff are discreet and even embarrassed at this point, but they must follow this procedure. Anything that is sharp, or can be made sharp by breakage will be confiscated. Similarly, all medicines or drugs will be removed so that the staff will have control over what you are taking, and other patients will not be able to get hold of them. At this point some units might put away your clothes and require you to wear a hospital gown, although this is not usual. This may be to prevent you from absconding, or be a part of the system of privileges which that ward uses. Other places will require that you be up and dressed at all times.

If you are considered to be in danger of hurting yourself, you will probably be placed under "close observation".

Close observation has different names, such as 'one to one', but it means that you are to be watched. You may be assigned a nurse who will escort you everywhere, even to the bathroom. Alternatively you might be required to remain in a specified area, which can be observed from the nurses' station. I have found that if the nurse is caring and intelligent, close observation can be a comforting thing. It does, however, isolate you from the other consumers, who will be a valuable source of help later on.

**You may feel bewildered, scared, or angry.
This is normal. Everyone does.**

At this point you may feel pretty desperate, and wonder how you ever allowed this to happen. Even on my ninth admission there seemed to me to be nothing so crushing as this amazing, fantastic reality that I was back in the hospital, and could no longer be at home with my husband and my dog. On this first day you have very few of your own things, and what you do have has been searched. This intensifies the sense of isolation. If you are allowed to, try to find out as much as you can from the other consumers — they know how you are feeling, they will explain the "system" to you, and may be of practical help in providing you with towels, items of clothing or whatever else you need. Resist the temptation to assume that you do not belong among all these "crazy people". They, like you, are ill, and you will find among them valuable and empathetic friends. I will never forget the companionship which I have received from the people in psychiatric wards.

**At your first meal, do not give away or
accept food from any other person. The
flatware may be plastic to prevent injury.**

In hospitals these days, food is invariably supplied on individual trays. The items are chosen by the consumer at least 36 hours before their preparation. As this is your first day you will be presented with a tray of food that you have not chosen and you will have to make the best of it. If you are ill with an eating disorder (ED) this will be of overwhelming significance to you and will be an added source of stress. You will be put on a strict regimen later, designed for your own needs, but on this first evening you can legitimately ask for help in trying to control your fear. I am grateful that this has never been an issue for me. One word of caution — unless you are sure that someone is not on an eating disorder regimen do not accept any food from him or her. Sometimes these consumers may use a hungry newcomer to dispose of food that they want to avoid eating. This deception will only cause that person distress, because if it is discovered, the lost calories will have to be "made up" with some form of supplement, and he or she will be dealt with sternly by the staff for the subterfuge. People in psychiatric wards are sometimes supplied with plastic flatware to prevent injury. Although this is a necessary precaution, it does hammer home the fact that you are no longer being treated as a responsible adult. During one of my stays there was a mix-up in the kitchen and we had real knives and forks. This mistake was a source of great hilarity to the less ill consumers, and of great concern to the nurses who bustled about counting cutlery at the end of the meal.

The rest of that day will feel like mere containment. That's what it is.

After the admission process you may be left to your own devices. There will probably be little to do, because your treatment program and activities have not yet been organized. The rest of that first day will feel like mere containment — which is exactly what it is. It is likely that you will not meet the doctor who will be in charge of your care until the next day. Now this day, your first in a psychiatric unit, stretches before you. This may be the worst day of your stay. You have to deal with the awful reality that you have officially joined the ranks of the mentally ill. Through no fault of your own, you have been admitted to a club to which you absolutely do not want to belong — and they will not let you leave.

As the day wears on, the reality of your situation will sink in. If you entered the hospital voluntarily, or on the advice of a trusted therapist, you will almost certainly doubt the wisdom of that decision, or the soundness of the advice. If you were hospitalized involuntarily you will probably be as mad as hell, unable to forgive the doctor who did this to you, and convinced that there has been some ghastly mistake or that you are the victim of some obscure plot. As bad as you feel, try to resist the urge to take it out on the nursing staff. They are not responsible for your being there, and are, in fact, just a group of human beings trying to do a job. As they are accustomed to abuse, especially from new patients, not being abused will be a refreshing change to them, so you can certainly influence the quality of the care you receive from them by your conduct. You may meet up with people who are convinced that the entire psychiatric profession is uniformly bad and ignorant, and uses the consumer merely to gratify some desire for power or money. These form the core of the anti-psychiatry movement whom I shall certainly offend by saying that I do not subscribe to this view. As with any other cross-section of humanity, the doctors and nurses you encounter will vary from the superb to the totally asinine. I have found that treating them all with equal courtesy results in an easier stay. This may be hypocritical, because I have met a few bad ones, but life in a psychiatric ward is hard enough without hostility from the staff. Similarly, do not antagonize the other consumers. These people are in pain, as you are, and deserve your respect. So, survival tactic number one — try not to hurt anyone.

You may start to feel very lonely. Try talking to the other consumers. Find out as much as you can.

After dinner, if you are not in bed or under constant supervision, you will have a chance to investigate your environment and find out about your fellow consumers. Relationships between consumers will be discussed later, but at this time, if you are a smoker, you will have to make some decisions. Due to the fact that access to shops is limited, even to those patients who have "outside privileges", commodities such as cigarettes are at a premium. If you do not have enough cigarettes on your first evening, you will usually find that most consumers who smoke will be willing to help out. However, your potential as a "bummer" will be rapidly assessed and the supply will soon dry up if you do not return their favors. Conversely, as a newcomer you will be approached as a potential source, and you will have to make decisions about whether or not to give cigarettes, and if so, to whom. You may be given a friendly warning about the established bummers of the ward. Recently some hospitals have become "smoke free zones" so, until you are allowed outside, you will find yourself suddenly deprived of nicotine completely, unless there is a designated smoking area. Nicotine patches may be prescribed to reduce your discomfort.

You will find, to your intense frustration if you are suicidal, that all the pictures are framed with plastic instead of glass, and that ashtrays, cups, etc. are all of some unbreakable material. Similarly the windows will be made of a type of advanced plastic which you cannot even break with a pick-ax. There are no bars now — although you may, if you are curious, find evidence of there once having been bars, by the small circles of different colored cement regularly spaced along the window-sills.

At night lying awake in the dark is awful.
If you can't sleep, get up and tell them.

So, bedtime approaches. Most wards have a set time for handing out night-time medications, after which you can go to bed. This is usually eagerly anticipated by many, because being asleep is better than being bored. If you are lucky, someone will have ordered a tranquilizer to help you sleep during your first night. If not you may have problems. Some night-staff look very unfavorably upon people getting up at night because it spoils their routine. Others, if things are quiet, will be quite amenable to talking with you, especially if you are scared, or providing hot drinks and magazines until you get sleepy. Many aspects of your stay depend on the personality and enthusiasm of the nurse on duty and that, inevitably, depends on the luck of the draw. If you are under close observation, a nurse will sit in the doorway of your room and your door will not be closed all night. If you are not to be closely watched you will nevertheless be observed, usually at half-hour intervals, by a nurse with a flashlight. Although this is for your protection it is not always conducive to a good night's rest.

The Next Morning

Try to shower and/or shave. After the effort, you will feel better.

When you wake on your first morning you may feel relieved that the night is over, and afraid of what is to come. What actually does happen next depends on the policy of the ward and on your level of privilege. Most places encourage people to be at least out of bed in time for breakfast, even if you cannot be dressed. If you are not allowed to wear your clothes you may still want to check out the showers. They will probably be locked and you will have to ask that they be opened, and that any confiscated items which you need be returned to you. Having to ask for your own things is not designed to feel humiliating — but it does, at least at first. If you were admitted only with what you were wearing, you may find that the others will help out with what you need. As a man you may find that the nurses can come up with a razor for you. If you are well enough, I cannot over-emphasize the difference that maintaining bodily care will make to your morale, and sense of dignity. Even when you are allowed only a hospital gown, if you have showered and/or shaved, I guarantee you will have a greater sense of control. It is a way of fighting — part of your arsenal.

When you take your shower, if you are under close observation your nurse will keep the door of the shower open and may talk to you during the process to elicit a response. If you are so ill that you are not even allowed to shower, you probably will not care anyway. When mental illness is that severe, mere existence feels so agonizing and complicated that deciding which sock to take off first seems overwhelming. I can remember being grateful that I was not allowed to dress, because it relieved me of having to decide how to get into my clothes.

**You will be interviewed again. Answer the
questions as honestly as you can no matter
how stupid they seem.**

Your next big hurdle is your interview with your doctor. Do
not expect to meet the same one as you did at your intake interview.
You will be faced with a stranger and will be expected to tell him or
her of the series of circumstances that resulted in your being there
that morning. This is painful and embarrassing. You may be very
angry or confused. You may not even know why you are there.

As before, I would stress that you be as honest as you can
and do not be surprised at having to tell the whole story again, and
in more detail. I do sincerely hope that you feel respected by your
doctor, and that you feel cared for as a person. If you do not like how
you feel about this person you cannot simply go elsewhere, as you
could outside — you have to try and work along with him or her as
best you can. Unfortunately this doctor has a lot of power over you,
as he or she will decide upon your course of treatment and level of
privilege. On the whole I have had good experiences with my
doctors. Only a small percentage were fools, and only one was an
outright crook. He wore shiny shoes and a three piece suit.
Consequently I distrust psychiatrists who wear shiny shoes. One of
the best ones I ever had turned up at our first meeting with odd
socks on. When I pointed this out, he grinned and said, "Yes, it's
been one of those days." I immediately trusted him for this total lack
of pretension. This made him human and approachable and he was
one of the kindest people I have ever met. I had an ally.

Conversely, one young resident who took care of me
responded to my question, "How are you?", with a snappish, "Let's
just stick to you, shall we?" I was only trying to treat him as a human
being, so why did he have to be so rude? It seemed as though he was
afraid of me because I did not abuse him. He always distrusted me
and I sensed that, throughout the entire time he took care of me. He
was, thankfully, an exception. Usually a doctor will appreciate your
courtesy and this will contribute to a mutual trust and respect and
will give you a sense of allegiance against the common enemy —
your illness.

**Limitations will be placed on you. Find out
what they are and do not exceed them. Get
the staff to trust you.**

You will find yourself starting to form relationships with the staff. The essential thing here, as in any human relationship, is a mutual respect and trust. If you feel that you are not respected as a person, then something is wrong. The staff also need to feel respected and, in order to be able to help you, they must be able to trust you. The reasons for my hospitalizations were basically because of self-destructive, even suicidal behaviors. These were usually precipitated by a Voice in my head telling me that, for various reasons, I should kill or injure myself. Consequently I was closely watched and asked to tell staff whenever these urges came upon me. They did not ask me not to hurt myself. I could not have promised that anyway. They only asked that I tell them when I had these feelings so that they could do their job of protecting me. I did want to make life easier for them, so I kept my promise although at times there was great conflict between my desire to obey the Voice, and the dictates of my conscience. So the staff learned to trust me; I was supervised less, and soon had more freedom and privileges. Therefore, even in a totally cold-hearted way, being as honest as you can with the staff does pay off, even though you may desperately want to do what your illness dictates to you. You also end up with friends, which always feels good. By allowing the staff to intervene on your behalf against your illness you will make faster progress, and go home sooner — you are not just earning "brownie points". Never pretend to be well when you are not. Simulating wellness may seem to be the way to a swift discharge, but it will blow up in your face when you find yourself outside, with your problems unsolved and your life more disrupted than ever by your having been away.

You will have to wait for your treatment to begin. Try to find something to do. If you cannot concentrate, talk to the other consumers.

Mental illness is one of the most isolating experiences there can be. The victim must suffer things which are very hard to share, and are not visible to the outsider. There may be thought distortion so that the victim cannot make sense of his environment. These cause the person to reject both himself and the idea that he might be ill.

Perhaps the single most important thing you can do for yourself is to overcome the self-rejection that you may feel at having been diagnosed as mentally ill. The other consumers understand this because they have had exactly the same battle as you. Finding friends and allies among them will help to break down your loneliness. They will be very happy to "clue you in" to the folklore of the ward, and warn you of the idiosyncrasies of various staff. Listen carefully to this. I have found that consumers are exquisitely perceptive, especially as to which staff are caring and respectful toward them. File this information away for future reference, but do also form your own opinions of the person concerned.

Start a written list of things that you want or need.

Another way to feel less isolated is to have some of your own things around you. Anything brought to you will be searched, so it helps to minimize the confiscation factor:
* use plastic containers instead of glass,
* do not have mirrors attached to anything,
* use emery boards instead of files or clippers,
* use electric shavers instead of razors,
* keep sharp things together in a strong transparent bag, clearly labeled with your name. They will still be confiscated, but are less likely to get lost.

As time passes, your list will change, but for now concentrate on the necessities — toiletries and clothes. The ward may have laundry facilities for its consumers, in which case you will need soap powder. Is there anything you particularly want, such as a favorite book or photograph? If you smoke, you will want a carton of cigarettes. Anything that can help you to feel better is, at this time, a valuable commodity.

The length of your stay

In the past, people have stayed in the hospital much longer than they do today, and this book was first written to help the person facing six to eight weeks on the ward. If you are discharged in less than a week, you can ignore the following information. If not, some of these things may be useful.

Learning to wait

After your interview, your doctor will decide on your course of treatment. This will take a little while for him or her to organize, so now you have to **wait**. You will get to be very good at it. Doctors and nurses are frequently late for their meetings with you. This feels as though they think you're not important. If you share this with the other consumers, you will find it happens to everyone.

You may be wondering how to get through the time. This depends upon your condition: each illness has its own barrage of difficulties, but there are still some problems that are shared by most consumers. The most common of these is an inability to concentrate, especially on reading. Only those who are almost ready for discharge will be seen reading. The more mechanical activities, such as knitting, come back sooner, but even these elude the ones who are really sick. This is extremely frustrating, especially if you are someone who is normally used to achieving a lot each day. A very good therapist once said to me: "If you had pneumonia, with a fever of 104°F, you would not expect to continue with your normal activities. This is an illness too, so be gentle with yourself." You may have a desire to pace about. This is so frequently resorted to by consumers that many modern units are designed like a racetrack so that you can go round and round, and still be observed from the nurses' station. If you are ill with an eating disorder and need to gain weight, pacing will be restricted because it burns calories. If you are on one-to-one, your nurse will probably be too exhausted to accompany you for long, and will make you sit down. Alternately, if you are so depressed that taking the next breath seems pointless, then all you will want to do will be to curl up in a fetal heap and stay that way for hours.

One form of activity that can help to pass the time is talking, either with your nurse, or with the other consumers. This alleviates the sense of isolation and you may even find yourself listening to the others and seeing that their symptoms are as bad as, or much worse than your own. You may encounter behavior in the others which alarms you at first. No one will be allowed to hurt you, and you can be fairly sure that if someone is nasty to you it is because that person either feels really awful himself, or is so disoriented that you are not actually a part of his world. I have found that most consumers have a great empathy for each other and, because they feel their backs are up against the wall, will share most of their possessions and experiences with you. Those who are allowed to go outside will bring things back for you, provided you return their favors when you can. If you are lucky you may find yourself forming powerful bonds with some of them. This can be a great help in making your stay more bearable — even, unbelievably, fun, for brief intervals.

Another undemanding activity which may be available to you is watching TV. In some units the TV is on all the time, in others it is limited to specified times. I have been confined for long periods to areas where the TV was on constantly, and I now have a loathing for day-time programming with its gruesome "soaps" and "real-life" talk shows. Another ubiquitous feature of psychiatric wards seems to be the ping-pong table. This encourages exercise in a way which is not dangerous, and the sound of this game will be in the background throughout your stay. It is, for me, forever associated with pain.

I have said many things to indicate that being in a psychiatric ward is no picnic, but it does have certain advantages, apart from the obvious one of getting better. You no longer have to struggle with your symptoms in order to appear "normal". There is always someone to go to if things get really bad. You have no responsibilities or decisions to make. You no longer have responsibility even for your existence. I have many times felt that I ought to kill myself. In the hospital this was virtually impossible, however, so I no longer felt guilty for continuing to live. The last and greatest benefit is, I think, that you are with other consumers, and you need no longer feel "odd". Meeting people with similar problems to your own allows you, suddenly, to feel recognized.

Choosing your food

After two days or so, you will find a menu sheet on your tray. The writers of these display a remarkable degree of creativity. After an investigation as to the nature of a "Peach Surprise" I was told, "Half a tinned peach in its own juice."

If you have an eating disorder, part of your treatment will be an introduction to the various food groups, and instructions on how to choose a balanced meal. Each unit will have its own procedures, but it is almost certain that you will not be allowed to choose your menu yet. As the subject of food is central to your illness, it will be central to your treatment. Your mealtimes will be closely monitored and you will find that your fellow sufferers will have developed sophisticated ways of disposing of food other than by eating it. Some of them will even boast about this when staff are not around. Whether or not you participate in these activities is up to you, but if you are discovered the staff will be quite strict with you. You may find that you are not allowed even to talk about food, calories, or weight while you are being supervised. Your eating behaviors will also be monitored; for instance "dicing" — or cutting food into very small pieces — is sometimes prohibited. All this sounds appalling to you now, and you will probably soon be angry and resentful that you are treated differently from the others. Most consumers with eating disorders do not, at first, accept that they even need to be in the hospital. You are facing a long hard battle, the hardest part of which will be changing your attitude to yourself. People with eating disorders frequently have to stay in the hospital much longer than those with other problems, an indication of how serious and intractable their illness is. This disease can kill you. Both the quantity and the quality of your life is at stake here. I can only encourage you to cooperate with the program as much as you can, so as to get back to a happy, fruitful life as soon as possible. "Fine for her to say," I can imagine you thinking, "she's never had to eat 3000 calories in a day." True, but I have seen my friends with this problem get well and go home.

Relationships with other consumers

You will, as I have mentioned, find good friends among your fellows. You may recognize yourself in them as you listen to their tales. You may even recognize their behaviors as things you do, or want to do. As I have said, I have been prone to self-injury in the past. The desire for this still comes to me when I am ill. When a friend of mine in hospital slashed her ankles, another person asked her why she would do that. She replied; "Because it hurts." He did not understand. I pointed out that it was an attempt to convert the internal pain which cannot be managed into something that you can put a bandage on. She immediately flung her arms around me, saying, "That's exactly right, Ginnie." This flash of recognition was wonderful for both of us. Conversely, when I found a depressed person who also heard voices telling her to jump under trains, it was very important to me. This symptom is not so very weird, it is just something the human brain does to itself when it is a little out of whack. I cannot over-emphasize the support and companionship I have received from psychiatric consumers.

Ward meetings

One thing which you may, or may not, encounter is the "ward meeting". I have been in units where there was no such thing, and in others where they were standard procedure. These meetings vary as to their intended purpose. Some may be another form of group therapy, while others are used as a forum for complaints or "issues" as they are called. They may be funny, useful or just plain boring. This depends on how they are conducted by the staff, and on the personalities of the consumers. Aggressive or insulting behavior is not permitted, and attendance is usually mandatory. The other consumers will tell you where and when they are held, and what you can expect from them.

You will hear a lot of "foul" language in a psychiatric unit and if you find this offensive it is a pity, but there is really nothing you can do. You are in the company of a population who really knows how to swear. To me language is only foul if it is intended to hurt someone, so this never bothered me. Consumers, on the whole, feel that they have plenty to swear about — so your vocabulary may be enlarged during your stay.

Black humor in the day-room

This will be an unexpected aspect of your hospital stay. This type of humor occurs only among those who are less ill, and usually when staff are not around. It takes the form of ridiculing the absurdity of the situations they share. Consumers almost never make fun of each other; there seems to be an unwritten law about that. However, they often make fun of their own problems. For instance, one friend of mine, confused after ECT, wandered into my room by mistake. She said to me, "Jeez, I'm so fucked up even the voices are hearing voices." Any ineptitude in the staff or system will be satirized unmercifully. Medical students are also fair game. I must confess to having made life difficult for one young man who was practicing his interviewing techniques on me. When he asked me to draw a clock-face, a standard test for spatial orientation, I asked, "Digital or analog?" to which he replied, "Digital." The psychiatrist in charge of this side-show intervened at that point. Any opportunity for harmless mirth is avidly seized upon by the consumer as a means of mere survival. Otherwise the situation would be so grim as to be intolerable. Laughter and jokes are usually encouraged by most of the staff, provided no one gets hurt.

Weekends and holidays

Finally, I would like to deal with the problems of weekends and holidays. I cannot find any printable words to describe these hellish times. They feel like something my dog would roll in. The doctors are all away, there is a minimal staff, most of whom don't want to be there anyway, and many of the consumers who would normally support you are out on "passes". As a newcomer, you will not be allowed any passes. Worse still, you may be deluged with well-intentioned visitors who now have time to see you. Unless they are among the enlightened few who are not afraid of mental illness, the things they say, and urge you to do, will seem irrelevant in the extreme. You may feel obliged to look "normal" or cheerful, in which case they will want to know why you are still "in here". This is especially so if you have children who visit you. If you are very ill, the efforts to seem "normal" may be beyond you, in which case you might not want them to see you at all. It's a tough decision, which only you can make. Let the staff help you with it — seeing you may frighten them, but not seeing you might be worse. All this must take into account their ages, personalities, and the quality of their relationships with you.

I have only one suggestion to offer, having never really solved these problems myself. It may be hard for you to concentrate, but games such as Scrabble or Trivial Pursuit, played with your visitors, do have the great advantage of substituting for conversation, and they also take the spotlight off you. Later, when you gain more privileges, you will be able to take them off the ward for trips to the cafeteria, etc. This eases their embarrassment, because they are no longer among "mental cases". They can even pretend to themselves that you are from a "normal" ward. Some people use this defense because the implications of someone they care about being "crazy" are too awful to contemplate. I will expand on this later. Off-ward excursions also divert the attention from you, which eases your embarrassment, and supply ample subjects for the conversation when it flags, as it undoubtedly will.

Your Legal Rights
A very basic discussion of your legal rights is presented as an appendix on page 73.

· 2 ·

Your Treatment

<u>Symptoms</u>

As I am not qualified to write about specific illnesses, I am going to write only about symptoms, and the types of treatment you may be offered to alleviate them. Let me stress the word "may". Who am I to tell you what type of treatment you should be given? This chapter is only intended to tell you what to expect — what the most common symptoms and their treatments are likely to feel like.

Most of these treatments have side-effects. I will describe how these feel and what can be done to minimize them. There are no wonder drugs. You will probably find yourself weighing symptoms against side-effects, and deciding which you prefer. The more awful your symptoms are, the more side-effects you are likely to put up with in order to be free of those symptoms. There are many ways in which side-effects can be reduced: alternative treatments may be available, doses can be adjusted, and medications can be used in combination to make you as comfortable as you can be. You are unlikely to have no side-effects, but if you are persistent, they can be managed.

Psychiatry is a field which changes very quickly, and some of what I say here will be out of date by the time you read it. However, many of the principles and feelings will not have changed, and that is the focus of this chapter.

The symptoms that trouble most consumers can be divided into four broad categories:

1) disorders of mood
2) anxiety
3) disorders of perception
4) obsessions and compulsions

This chapter will be divided into four sections, corresponding to these categories. In each section the symptoms will be described, in terms of what they are, how they feel, and most important of all — what they can make you do. The treatments offered for each type of symptom will also be listed, with notes on how they feel; their side-effects, and what you can do about them. In this way you can find what you want quickly, without having to read material that may be irrelevant, or even alarming to you.

<u>Medication — some general notes</u>

In order to be effective, a medicine must reach, and remain at, a certain concentration in the blood for a certain period of time. Obviously, if you are a large person, with a large blood volume, you are going to need more medicine to attain this desired "therapeutic" concentration than if you are tiny. Other factors, such as the efficiency of your metabolism, any other medicines you are taking, and your nutritional state, will also affect the time it takes for your medication to be effective. Generally, you will be started with a low dose, your response will be monitored, and the dose adjusted until the therapeutic level is reached. Some medications, at higher doses, can have a "paradoxical" effect and can make the symptom they were intended to alleviate, worse. It so happens that the anti-anxiety medication, Buspar, at high doses, causes me to have extreme anxiety. Therefore it is absolutely essential that you be totally honest with your doctor about how you feel.

The unfortunate fact is that almost always, the side-effects manifest themselves immediately, while you have to wait for the desired "effect" to occur. This interlude is very discouraging. This is the time when you need most support, and a good relationship with your doctor is essential. Consumers who have not been able to establish a rapport with the staff have a worse time at this point, and I think that this is the time when much of the disillusionment about psychiatry sets in. You may hear the less tolerant of your companions complaining bitterly about the fact that the pills are not helping them, but just make them feel bad physically.

You may come across consumers who are vehement in their denigration of all medications. They may tell you that medications are poisonous, that being medicated only masks your problems, or that you will be a zombie for the rest of your life. These things are real concerns for them, but they may not be helpful to you. I recently had a conversation with a young man who had decided not to take medication, because he had been told that it would take away his creativity. He had recently made a serious attempt to take his own life. I wanted to point out to him that one cannot be very creative from the grave, and that, because of his depression, he had all but stopped working on his novel. He is missing a possible avenue of help because of what he had heard. Each instance of mental illness is as unique as the person it afflicts: there is no paved highway to wellness, we each have to find our own way. Your way may, or may not include medication, but you have very little to lose by trying it. You can always stop taking it — you are not irrevocably trapped in that mode for the rest of your life. So do not be frightened by the horror stories you will hear. Be guided by your own mind, and what your body tells you.

Do not be disturbed or afraid if you have symptoms which are described in more than one category — most of us do. Similarly you may well be offered more than one medication. Often medications work better together, and a smaller dose of each is required. This is a good way of reducing their side-effects. Do not assume that the more pills you take, the more ill you must be. The feelings you have about taking medication, are very important, and will be dealt with more fully in Chapter 4.

Another important aspect of this subject is withdrawal. Coping strategies for changes in your medication regimen will be discussed at the end of this chapter.

Section 1) Disorders of Mood

The symptom most often encountered in psychiatric wards is depression. Clinical depression may be your major symptom, or it may be part of whatever else you suffer from, but it is not just feeling "fed-up", as you will know if you have experienced it. In Darkness Visible[1] William Styron suggests that there should be a special word for clinical depression to distinguish it from feeling "blah" on a Monday morning. I agree wholeheartedly with this. No one who has not suffered this can really conceive of its intensity. Unfortunately, all of us occasionally feel blue, so some people think that they do know what clinical depression feels like, when in fact they do not. There are few things more demoralizing than to be told "everyone gets depressed", after you have just screwed up the courage to tell someone about your problem. So the victim may be actively discouraged from seeking help by well-meaning, but misinformed relatives or friends. Phrases like, "It's all in your head," or "You think too much," bounce around the victim's mind, so that the person may start to believe that he or she deserves to feel this bad.

Depression is hell. It's like a sandstorm in an icy desert. The victim is isolated; unable to participate in any normal activity. Nothing, not even things which were formerly pleasant to the person, can be enjoyed, and everything is pain. Very often sleeping and eating patterns are disturbed, so the body is deprived of the basic things it needs, and the victim feels physically unwell. Perhaps the hardest part of this is the sense that everything is pointless, and that this pain will never end. People often feel that seeking help is useless, because the idea of ever feeling better seems like an impossible dream.

Depression can make you kill yourself. Fifteen per cent[2] of its untreated victims die by suicide, so it is an illness with a very high mortality. If you have ever thought that suicide might be a possibility for you then GET HELP. I cannot stress this too highly — it is a real illness, and not to be toyed with.

The opposite of depression is mania. I have never fully experienced this, but friends tell me that it brings feelings of omnipotence, infinite energy, there is no need for sleep, and that everything is possible. The inhibitions that normally govern the way we think and act are reduced. This may lead to associations between ideas which are usually disparate. If they are not destructive, these associations can be very intriguing and original — creative artists have a higher incidence of mania than does the normal population. Thoughts seem to follow fast upon each other, the person becomes highly distractible, and is so anxious to express these ideas that his or her speech is "pressured".

Sadly, we need these same inhibitions for prudent behavior, and without them the victim may spend large amounts of money, become promiscuous, or start outlandish business ventures that are doomed to failure. This often has dire consequences, not only for the person in pain, but also for the family, which may be bankrupted as a direct result of these symptoms. In the hospital, manic people are usually very talkative, energetic, restless, and given to interrupting others' conversations. They may also make embarrassing requests. One friend of mine became manic, and at times he would realize what he was doing and start weeping and apologizing, saying, "I'm not really like this, I don't know what's happening to me." So, although mania is popularly associated with euphoria, it actually contains much pain and confusion.

One word which you might hear is "hypomania". This means "below mania", and many consumers have told me that it feels wonderful. They have all the energy and enthusiasm that mania brings, need very little sleep, and can successfully do several things at once. Yet they are still in touch with reality, and do not do the inappropriate things that come with mania. Many people function admirably in this mode for years before they have their first full-blown attack of mania. They are not aware of any problem until this occurs. When they are medicated, to stabilize their mood, they may resent the treatment, because it prevents them from being hypomanic, and they feel dull and lifeless.

A number of antidepressants are listed in the Table 1a. Mania is treated with mood stabilizers. ECT is still used for depression, and it is fully described. Cognitive and supportive psychotherapy is useful for mood disorders, especially for developing your own ways of coping if the demon starts to rear its ugly head again.

Table 1a. Antidepressants[3,4]

Type of Drug	Brand name (generic name)	Common side-effects
Tricyclic	Anafranil (clomipramine)*	Lethargy
	Aventyl (nortriptyline)	Constipation
	Elavil (amitriptyline	Urine retention
	Norpramin (desipramine)	Weight gain
	Sinequan (doxepin)	
	Surmontil (trimipramine)	
	Triptil (protriptyline)	
	Tofranil (imipramine)	
MAOIs	Parnate (tranylcypromine)	Restricted diet
	Nardil (phenelzine)	Interactions with OTC medicines
	Mannerix (maclobemide)	See below
SSRIs		Hyperactivity,
	Luvox (fluvoxamine)	decreased appetite
	Paxil (paroxetine) *	weight loss,
	Prozac (fluoxetine) *	insomnia, and
	Zoloft (sertraline) *	sexual dysfunction
Others	Asendin (amoxapine)	Individual response
	Effexor (venlaxafine)	varies widely.
	Ludiomil (maprotyline)	Consult a detailed
	Serzone (nefazodone)	text for specific
	Wellbutrin(bupropion)	information

* this medicine has been approve for OCDs. (Section 4)

Table 1b. Mood stabilizers.[3 ; 4]

Type of Drug	Brand names (generic name)	Common side-effects
lithium salts	Lithane, Eskalith, Lithobid Lithotabs (lithium)	Excessive thirst tremor water retention Needs frequent blood measurement
Others	Napakine (valproic acid) Tegretol (carbamazepine)	Indigestion, tremor, menstrual changes, weight gain Clumsiness, drowsiness, light headedness, nausea

To the best of our knowledge, antidepressants work by improving the efficiency of communication between your brain cells — they can talk to each other more easily. Different types of antidepressants do this in different ways, and that is why they vary in the types of side-effects they cause.

Tricyclics

A frequently used type of antidepressant — one of which I take myself — is the tricyclic, so called because of its chemical structure. The most common side-effects of these are: sedation and feelings of exhaustion, dry mouth, constipation, urinary retention, and feeling dizzy if you stand up too fast. There are other more obscure effects which occur in special cases, for example, glaucoma may be aggravated, so please describe everything you feel to your doctor. I never really found an effective cure for the sedation, except that a regular exercise program seems to help. The dry mouth can be a real problem if you have to talk for any length of time. It is surprising how hard it is to articulate when you do not have any spit. But there are ways to cope. Sugar-free gum is a good standby; it should be sugar-free because, as you have very little saliva, your teeth will be more prone to develop cavities. Recently, moisture sprays have become available; these feel a bit "gluey" but they are very portable, and can help when you have no access to fluids. The best solution is to drink lots of water or sugar-free soda because this will also help with the constipation and urinary retention. Many of the psychoactive medications cause constipation, and I think it is a problem which should be dealt with more aggressively than it is, by professionals. The consumer is often left to ask for help over this and when people are very depressed it is too much to expect them even to recognize it.

Urinary retention is more of a frustration than a problem. You may find it hard to start, and maintain your flow of urine. Listening to running water and thinking about waterfalls can help, but the best solution is to drink lots of fluids so that your bladder is constantly flushed out. When urine is retained in the bladder, an ideal environment is created in which bacteria can multiply, so the possible complications of this side-effect are urinary tract infections. If you keep up a good intake of fluids you are less likely to encounter this problem.

The last common side-effect that I mentioned was dizziness after standing up too fast. This becomes less of a problem with time, but it never goes away completely. Even now, when I am engrossed in browsing through books on the lowest shelf in a store, I forget about this and I often have to cling to the shelves for a moment when I stand up.

I included weight gain in the table, because it is listed in the books. However, it is not inevitable, and many people do not have this problem.

MAOI antidepressants

Another type of antidepressant that is commonly used is the MAOI. This stands for "monoamine oxidase inhibitor". This type is often used when the tricyclics have failed or when other problems, such as panic attacks, are present. The main drawback of the MAOIs is that certain foods must be avoided which contain a chemical called tyramine. These include herring, beer, aged cheese, and yogurt. Amphetamines, cocaine and hay-fever pills must also be avoided. If a person taking an MAOI does ingest these things there is the risk of a "hypertensive crisis". This means that your blood pressure soars and you get a splitting headache, with fever and vomiting. The reason for this is that the MAOIs prevent your body from processing tyramine and, when left unchanged in your system it can cause these frightening symptoms. Some people do not find these restrictions troublesome, but if you are habituated to cocaine or beer, then you will have to make some adjustments, and if something else works for you then you may think that the MAOIs are more trouble than they are worth.

One new MAOI, Mannerix, does not require dietary restrictions, but may not be as useful for treating depression which is accompanied by other problems, as are the older MAOIs.

SSRI antidepressants

In the past ten years, new antidepressants have been introduced which, for some, have revolutionized the treatment of depression. I refer to the controversial Prozac, and its newer cousins, Paxil and Zoloft. The term SSRI refers to the way in which these medicines work to improve the communication between your nerve cells — it is different from the tricyclics and the MAOIs. Hence the side-effects of these are very different from the other antidepressants, and many people find them much easier to live with. It is a shame that Prozac has received such bad press, as it must deter people from trying something that could be a real source of help to them.

The SSRIs do not cause sedation, and so you do not feel too tired to participate in activities that would help to make you feel better. The SSRIs can make you hyperactive, and cause anxiety, so you might feel in need of a mild sedative. For me, a small dose of Buspar, with Prozac works very well. Other minimal side-effects are nausea and insomnia: these can be reduced by taking the whole dose first thing in the morning, with a light breakfast.

The side-effects of the "other" antidepressants are many and varied. This does not mean that they are severe. People respond very differently to any medication. Please consult one of the books on medications listed in my bibliography, and discuss your symptoms thoroughly with your doctor.

Mood Stabilizers

Mania is usually treated with lithium, which is looked upon as a mood stabilizer, rather than a depressant. It does not have any really terrible side-effects in most people, provided the lithium concentration in the blood does not rise too high. Therefore lithium blood concentration must be constantly monitored by taking blood samples, usually every two weeks. The necessity for this monitoring is because lithium can cause nausea, vomiting, excessive urination, and kidney damage if its concentration in the blood rises too high.

Psychotherapy

While I firmly believe in a biochemical basis for mental illness, there is much to be said for examining your life-style to see if some changes could be made which would lessen the frequency, and intensity of your symptoms. These adjustments may be in physical matters such as changing your job, or getting out of an unhappy marriage; or they may be in attitudinal matters such as choosing friends who do not hurt you, or rearranging the way you think about yourself. Something fairly drastic must have happened to necessitate your hospitalization. The causes of your distress may have started years ago, and the changes necessary to alleviate it may take years to accomplish. The role of the hospital is to get you well enough to start to consider what must be done, and to return you to an environment in which you can be safe. There simply is not time for effective long-term psychotherapy in the hospital milieu. The resident taking care of you probably feels like a tired brain on legs, and his or her role is largely to prescribe medications for you and monitor your response. Ideally, part of the nurses' role is to talk to you, but this is chiefly to assess the way you feel, and report these symptoms to the doctor. Simply talking to a nurse, when you are in acute distress, is comforting, especially if he or she is wise and receptive. Such an interchange is a form of psychotherapy; but really its aim is to console you, allow you to see that changes must be made, and give you the beginnings of the strength you need to make them.

Effective psychotherapy takes place outside the hospital when you are intact enough to stand up to the stress that change always causes. For this to be helpful a very special bond has to develop between the therapist and the patient. It may be the most intimate relationship you have ever experienced. This does not happen with just anybody; and it certainly does not occur when you talk to a different nurse each day, or a resident who, however well-intentioned, has a thousand other things to do. The best you can hope for is a respectful, caring environment in which you can recover sufficiently to leave the hospital. Then you can go out and find that special therapist, with whom you can form this bond and examine the possibilities for your better mental health. As I have stated, you cannot "shop-around" in the hospital. If you are fortunate enough to feel drawn toward a certain nurse or social worker, you cannot work with that person on a long-term basis, unless he or she sees patients outside the hospital. The type of psychotherapy you will encounter in the hospital will be short-term and intense. It is intended to get you well enough to live in the real world again, at which point you will be strongly advised to find someone with whom you can work on your problems.

Unfortunately, sometimes this short-term, intense type of therapy can misfire. During one of my earlier hospitalizations it was deemed advisable to make me angry. Early in the week, I was promised passes for both Saturday and Sunday, during which I could spend time with my husband. We were both eagerly anticipating this, and made plans as to where we would go. I clung to the prospect of the coming weekend and I ironed all my clothes in honor of the occasion. On Friday afternoon my passes were revoked on the facile excuse that I needed to "work on some issues" with my nurse. It was a deliberate, and I suppose well-intentioned, ploy to anger me. For me, it was probably the most painful disappointment I have ever experienced: instead of getting angry I became monumentally depressed and, by Sunday, had decided that the doctor was quite correct — it was appropriate that I should be treated in that way, as a punishment for being such a worthless person. It set me back by weeks. The hospitalized consumer is easy prey to practices such as that just described, at a time when he or she is already terribly vulnerable. This type of incident justifiably fuels the wrath of the anti-psychiatry movement.

<u>Light Therapy</u>

This may be offered to you if your depressions appear to be seasonal. If you feel more depressed in the autumn and winter, and your mood improves with the lengthening days of spring, you may have what is called "seasonal affective disorder" (SAD). During light therapy the consumer must receive a certain quantity of light each day, usually in the early morning. This is achieved by the person sitting in front of a fluorescent light for a prescribed time. The apparatus has a filter to remove UV rays, and the person is instructed not to look directly into the lights. The time required is dependent upon the brightness of the light — with brighter lights less exposure is needed. It is not yet known what component of the light is therapeutic in SAD[5], neither have the long term side-effects yet been fully investigated. The short-term side-effects include eyestrain and headaches, feeling "wired", and nausea[6]. One might also include boredom, although even that has been alleviated by the production of a baseball-type hat which has small lights under the peak which shine into your eyes, and you can wear this for a set period each day while you do other things. The usual trial period is two weeks, because light therapy works within days, on the appropriate type of consumer.

<u>Electroconvulsive therapy (Shock Treatments)</u>

The treatment offered for mood disorders as a last resort is electroconvulsive therapy (ECT). It is also sometimes used for catatonic schizophrenia. Anyone who has seen <u>One Flew Over the Cuckoo's Nest</u> is perfectly justified in being scared silly at the prospect of ECT. Modern methods, however, have eliminated much of the suffering involved in this treatment, although, after two series of ECT, even I would be alarmed if a doctor wanted to use it on me again. There seem to be many myths attached to this controversial treatment, amongst both consumers and doctors. Firstly, although it seems like mending a computer with a sledge-hammer, ECT does not cause any detectable permanent brain damage. It does however, cause great confusion in the consumer, both immediately after the treatment, and to a lesser extent, for about six months afterwards. This may account for the suspicions the layman has, about its lasting effect on the brain. As for professional myths, I have read two

accounts of ECT written by separate MDs in which one stated that;
"Five minutes [after the shock] the patient awakes from the
anesthesia, alert and without pain. The patient does not remember
the shock or complain of discomfort."[7] The other account states that,
"None, as far as I could tell, had any discomfort other than the effect
of the general anesthetic."[8] This makes me angry, because neither of
these doctors have received ECT three times a week for six weeks.
As one of my friends put it, "These shock treatments really knock the
shit out of me." She was not a complainer, but was weeping
uncontrollably at the time. It is true that ECT is much less invasive
than open heart surgery, or even some of the more potent psychoactive medications; it is also true that ECT works in many cases of
both mania and depression, where nothing else has helped. Let us
not, however, be under any illusions: for sheer discomfort ECT
probably ranks right up there alongside having impacted wisdom
teeth removed — once or twice might be okay, but to know that you
are facing confusion, probable nausea and vomiting, and the worst
headache you can imagine, three times a week for six weeks, is a real
test of character. So, as a consumer you have a perfect right to be
afraid, and to ask if there might not be an alternative.

Now that I have got that off my chest, I must add that if
nothing else helps, and your doctor recommends ECT, then do
please try it. I have seen it help friends of mine and it may help you.
I am trying here to give a balanced and non-hysterical account of a
procedure which has received much bad press, because of its
indiscriminate and unsophisticated use in the past. I will now
outline, from the consumer's point of view, each stage of the
procedure, so that you will know what to expect — I hope this will
make it less frightening for you.

On the day of your ECT you will be required to wear a
hospital gown, and you will not be allowed anything to eat or drink.
A nurse or technician will come and set up an intravenous line (IV)
in your arm to keep you hydrated and so that medicines can easily
be introduced into your bloodstream. One of these will be atropine,
to dry up your saliva and prevent irregular heart rhythms. This part
is usually done on your own ward, and you will then have to wait
until the ECT department is ready for you. This waiting period is
both tedious and nerve-racking. When they are ready for you, the

ECT department will call your ward and a nurse will take you to them, and remain with you throughout the procedure. The ECT room looks and smells like an operating room. You will be asked to lie on a stretcher, and they will check that you have no false teeth or contact lenses in. Disks, to monitor your heart, will be stuck onto various places on your chest and back — you may find them still there when you wake up. A conductive gel will be applied to your forehead, either in the middle and to one side — unilateral ECT — or to both sides — bilateral ECT. Electrodes, that feel like smooth metal disks will be placed into this gel, and held in place with a wide rubber band around your head. <u>Do not freak out</u>. They are not going to shock you while you are still awake; placing the electrodes at this point is to minimize the amount of time that you have to be anesthetized. An oxygen mask will be placed over your nose and mouth, and you will be given, via your IV, a short-acting anesthetic to put you to sleep, and a muscle relaxant to prevent you from thrashing about and injuring yourself. You will not be aware of the shock that is administered, and your "convulsion" will only appear as a spike in the electroencephalograph that is monitoring your brain function — or so I am told. When you wake up you will be very confused, you will have an awful headache, and you may take the rest of that day to recover. I always did, but I have friends who were up and about after only two hours. During the actual course of the treatments you will not store many memories, so that period will always be hazy to you. I had episodes of confusion for about six months after the last ECT.

So, there you have it. It is no walk in the park, but if your depression is intractable, and the staff are concerned for your safety, then it may just save your life. ECT is not fun, but it does work, and these days is not used indiscriminately or to punish or intimidate you.

Section 2. Anxiety

We all suffer from anxiety as part of our everyday existence, and having any psychiatric disorder is a good reason to be anxious. Usually anxiety is not the main problem, but is caused by whatever else the person must endure. Sometimes, however, anxiety is itself the chief source of pain; the person is not "anxious about" a specific thing, but is anxious in a global, all-encompassing way. The normal symptoms of anxiety with which we are all familiar, become so intense as to be disabling, so that the person becomes helpless, and feels out of control.

Such anxiety is treated in a variety of ways, depending upon its source, and severity. Relaxation techniques, and stress management are offered for mild or "normal" anxiety, but when it is severe, antianxiety and sedative medications are used, along with antidepressants and psychotherapy.

Table 2. Antianxiety and sedative medications.[3 ; 4]

Drug Type	Brand name (generic name)	Common side-effects
Benzo-diazapines	Ativan (lorazepam)	Drowsiness
	Halcion (triazolam)	Dizziness
	Restore (temazepam)	Weakness
	Rivotril (clonazepam)	Constipation
	Serax (oxazepam)	All are addictive
	Tranxene (clorazepate)	to some degree
	Valium (diazepam)	
	Xanax (alprazolam)	
Barbiturates	Amytal (amobarbital)	Drowsiness
	Nembutal (pentobarbital)	Dizziness
	Seconal (secobarbital)	Clumsiness
Others	Buspar (busparone)	Drowsiness Dizziness, dry mouth Headache

Barbiturates are still used in special circumstances, such as just before surgery, or in the treatment of seizures, but in recent years they have been replaced by the benzodiazapines for the treatment of anxiety. The big drawback with these is that they are all addictive to a greater or lesser degree, and should not be used indiscriminately. If your symptoms are terrifying you or you suffer from extreme anxiety, then being sedated while in the hospital is a good temporary measure until alternatives can be found that will help you. It is very difficult to try to function outside the hospital if you are heavily sedated — simple things, like crossing a road, become major obstacles. These medications also cause constipation, but do not dry your mouth or cause urinary retention.

Our culture is saturated with material on stress, and how to manage it, and I am sure that if you have come this far, you will already have had some experience with it. Sometimes, biofeedback is offered so that you can monitor your own responses, and learn how to be more effective in whatever techniques you are using. Learning these methods does take time and patience, and the process can seem extremely futile, especially if you have lived with stress for a long time. However, even if they do not completely eliminate your symptoms, relaxation techniques can help insofar as you may be able to use less medication when you have mastered them. Also, they are available to you at any time, you do not need a drug plan, they do not have side-effects, and best of all, you control when and how you use them. This sense of control is very important, and I will expand upon that theme in Chapter 6.

Section 3. Disorders of Perception

Other painful symptoms that consumers often have to cope with are those of delusions and hallucinations. Delusions are, "...fixed false beliefs, not open to logical persuasion, and lacking the consensual validation of culture"[9]. This means that the victim believes something about his or her life that everyone else sees cannot be true. This sometimes seems funny to others, but to the victim it is painful in the extreme. For instance, I was once convinced that something had gone "philosophically wrong" with the Universe because I was born. I was truly convinced that, if I killed myself everything would be all right in the world. I also believed that I took up too much space, ate too much food, and breathed too much oxygen. Now that may sound hilarious, but for me it was a dreadfully painful thing to live with, and entirely disruptive to normal life. So please be gentle if you encounter someone with this type of problem — for that person, it is real and awful.

Hallucinations are "sensory perceptions occurring in the absence of external stimuli"[9]. The most common of these is hearing voices that others cannot hear. False perceptions can occur in the other senses, but less frequently in my experience. In the next chapter I will describe my brief encounter with these demons. As with delusions, the extent of damage that hallucinations can cause depends largely on how the consumer responds to them. For instance, I used to hear a Voice telling me to injure myself. If, at that point, I was sufficiently in touch with reality to know that what She said was not a good idea, then She could not actually harm me. It was painful to have Her around, but fundamentally I was safe. If, however, I became sick enough actually to believe Her, then I was in danger.

Hallucinations can literally be life-threatening. I once knew a man who saw his food turn to live worms whenever he tried to eat. He was brought into the hospital because he was starving, and he had to be fed intravenously for several weeks until his psychosis had cleared. It was pitiful to watch him trying to eat with his eyes closed. Without help he would have died. So I would like to emphasize again the need for total honesty with your doctor. If you think you are perceiving something that other people are not, then check it out and <u>tell</u> someone. When I was first in treatment, I took three months to tell my therapist about the Voice, because I thought he would not believe me — the Voice told me he would not — and would refuse to see me any more. He could not understand my obvious distress and lack of improvement. When I did finally tell him, we were both relieved; he, because it explained my behavior, and I, because he became my ally against the Voice, and the things she told me to do. Consumers accept and understand the concept of hallucinations — they are discussed and compared in a matter-of-fact way, as one would compare cars. One evening toward the end of my last hospitalization, an illuminated blimp flew over the city, advertising a new type of pizza. I saw it from my window, and went quickly to the day room to check that the others could see it as well. No one laughed at me — to them it was a perfectly reasonable concern.

The most dreadful aspect of these symptoms is that they isolate the patient. The symptoms are bad enough, but to know that you are the only person to be aware of them, means that you are really, totally alone. I have described the relief which I felt when I discovered that someone else on my ward heard voices telling her to jump under trains. The other aspect of this problem is the fear it carries. To find out that you are hallucinating, might mean you are "really going crazy", with all the terrifying implications that such a concept carries in our society.

Delusions and hallucinations are treated with a wide variety of antipsychotics and sedatives. Psychotherapy is also offered, but it is of limited value until these symptoms are controlled. These medications have a wide variety of side-effects and in general enjoy a poor reputation among consumers. The side-effects are often preferable to the symptoms, however. They do work effectively to subdue hallucinations and, in doing so, can at least return you to some grasp of reality. Antipsychotics have a strange effect on the parts of your nervous system that control your muscles. The doctors call this "akathisia" which means that you are restless — when you are standing you want to sit, when you are sitting you want to stand or pace about. One kindly Belgian doctor once asked me, "And do you have an impatience in your legs?" which I thought was a very good way of putting it. At the same time as you want to move about,

Table 3. Antipsychotic medications[3,4]

Drug Type	Brand name (generic name)	Common side-effects
Classic antipsychotics	Mellaril (thioridazine)	Dry mouth,
	Haldol (haloperidol)	hypotension,
	Serentil (mesoridazine)	akathesia,
	Thorazine (chlorpromazine)	constipation,
	Loxapac (loxapine)	urine retention,
	Orap (pimozide)	drowsiness, and
	Prolixin (fluphenazine)	tardive
	Stelazine (trifluoperazine)	diskynesia
	Trilafon (perphenazine)	
Novel agents	Risperdal (risperidone)	Dry mouth,
	Zyprexa (olanzapine)	hypotension,
	Seroquel (quetiapine)	akathesia,
		constipation,
		urine retention, and drowsiness. However, less risk of TD (no long term data available yet)
	Clozaril (clozapine)	Dry mouth, hypotension, quite sedating, and little or no akathesia. Low risk of TD

you will also find yourself becoming stiff in your joints so that you walk with a characteristic slow gait, and you feel trapped. You want to move normally but something prevents you from doing so. Your speech may also be impaired, and if things have reached that point then you will probably feel so sedated that none of this really matters to you any more. Consequently, you will not be likely to seek help, and it is up to your doctor to watch for these signs. There is a medication, Cogentin, which can rapidly alleviate this discomfort, and it is often prescribed along with the antipsychotic as a standard procedure. Unfortunately, Cogentin has the effect of causing blurred vision, and you may need a pair of drug-store reading glasses during the time that you are on this regimen. There are also the side-effects of dry mouth, constipation, and urinary retention which I have already discussed.

It does sound like fun, doesn't it? Someone who has not experienced the dreadfullness of a full-blown psychosis might say, on reading this, that they would never accept such a regimen: but, awful as these things sound, they are preferable to some of the horrors to which the human brain can subject itself. You would only be given such medicine if you really needed it, and for a limited period of time. Long-term use of antipsychotics (i.e. years) can cause permanent damage to your nervous system in the form of tardive dyskinesia, (TD) which is emphatically to be avoided. This is a syndrome in which you make involuntary and jerky movements with your face and mouth. If it is caught in time, withdrawal of the medication can cure it, but the symptoms can persist even after the drug has been removed. You will hear the other consumers discuss the syndrome, and you may even encounter an older person who has it permanently. In those unfortunate people whose symptoms are so awful and intractable that their only options are to take antipsychotics or live in terrified seclusion, then even TD is an acceptable risk.

Section 4. Obsessions and Compulsions

An obsessions is "an idea or thought that intrudes itself persistently into one's consciousness."[10] Usually the person is plagued by the thought that he or she is a source of danger to others. Such thoughts are hard to live with, and often lead to compulsive acts, which are intended to lessen the danger. For example, a person may feel sure that he or she is a source of infection. That person may feel compelled to reduce the sense of threat by washing repeatedly, or using powerful and dangerous disinfectants on his or her body. This can lead to terrible physical damage, for instance if the victim bathes in Lysol concentrate. If someone spends more than one hour per day on this compulsive activity, then he or she is said to have obsessive-compulsive disorder (OCD).

Recently, four of the antidepressants listed in Table 1a have been approved for the treatment of OCDs. These are Anafranil, a tricyclic, and three of the SSRIs; Prozac, Paxil, and Zoloft. These are discussed in Section 1.

Behavior Modification

The method of treatment known as "behavior modification" is based on B. F. Skinner's theory of operant conditioning which states that: "behavior is an overt response that is externally caused and is primarily caused by its consequences"[11]. The consumer is seen only as a set of responses which can be manipulated by reward and punishment, to suit the requirements of the staff. This narrow concept allows no room in the person for emotions, ambitions, or the ability to reason, and is justifiably out of vogue. You are unlikely to hear the term "behavior modification" in a modern psychiatric environment. The concept, however, is still at work in most treatment programs, and, in that context, is no bad thing. For instance, during my treatment, when I reported that I was experiencing the urge to injure myself, I was rewarded by the approval and attention of a staff member. Had I thought that they did not care whether I was injured or not, then the momentary relief of the act of self-harm would have been my reward, and that piece of behavior would then remain unchanged. So I can say that I have been subject to behavior modification.

Similarly, the compulsive slowness in eating that plagues sufferers of anorexia, is sometimes treated by timing their meals. In one unit I know of these consumers are required to finish a meal within one hour. If they do not, they must then finish it in seclusion. In the modern setting, however, such a system is not used in a vacuum; the issues relating to the desire for negative behavior are also addressed, the pain itself is treated with appropriate medications, and the patient's life situation is also examined. So, modern behavior modification is usually only part of the many ways in which the whole person is treated.

The universal side-effect

There is one last side-effect to which I want to give a special discussion. This is the question of your sexual potency. The psycho-active medications all seem to have some effect on this, and other consumers will tell you of their various misadventures when they know you well enough. This problem is not dangerous or painful but it is a major frustration, and its consequences are psychological rather than medical, seeming to be far worse for men than for women. If you are very ill and your life is so obscured by pain that you never even think about sex, then the inability to be aroused or reach an orgasm will not bother you. Impotence may not even matter much if you are sexually active, so long as you do not blame yourself, or regard it as a failing on your part. If you do, however, attach a great deal of importance to your sexual performance, then the lack of it may become a serious source of distress, and it is worth at least asking your doctor about possible alternatives.

Changes in your medications

Much has been written about what to expect when you start to take a certain medication. I have yet to see a comprehensive account of what to expect when you stop. This is a very important subject, and one that is often dismissed as unimportant by professionals.

Some people are able to tolerate changes in their regimen without any noticeable consequences. As I have stated, each of us is unique in the way we respond to treatment. I have found that I am very sensitive to changes in my dose, and I think it important to address this aspect of therapy.

First, you should know that even if your medication is not addictive, your nervous system has adjusted to its presence, and any change is likely to make you <u>feel different</u>. I am not saying that changes are difficult or undesirable, but you must expect some consequences. The higher your dose, and the longer you have used the medication, the more likely you are to have a reaction to change. While I am loathe to use the term "withdrawal" because of the connotations it has, that is as good a word as any to describe what happens when your medication is reduced. Sometimes you will feel better for the first few hours, and only after the medication level drops, will you start to feel strange. The best way to make a change, is very, very slowly, but this is sometimes not possible, as, for example, when I needed to stop taking Mellaril, because I was showing the first signs of TD.

The adjustment might feel a bit like having 'flu; you might sweat profusely, or feel as though there are insects crawling through your limbs. Sounds and colors may seem especially bright. The best way to cope with this, is to drink a lot of water, take some gentle exercise, and be aware that it will not last forever. Do not plan to do anything very demanding, and try not to be afraid — this is a natural reaction.

If you are prepared for this process, it is much less alarming, than if you do not know what is happening to you, and think you are really ill. Unfortunately, the professionals are sometimes reluctant to acknowledge that this happens, and do not warn you in advance. So, when your regimen is to be changed, do ask them what to expect, and what can be done about it.

· 3 ·

If You Are Terribly Ill

"You lock the door, and throw away the key.
There's someone in my head, but it's not me."
Pink Floyd; Dark side of the Moon.

A. Surviving Your Survival

So, you tried to die. Many of us do. I did and almost succeeded. Psychiatric illness is unique in that suicide is the major cause of death among its victims. This may be why mental illness carries the stigma that it does, but I think there is more to it than that. I firmly believe that the reasons you had for your attempt were valid to you at the time. Suicide is a powerful statement, but it says different things to different people. I have often heard expressions of contempt for the suicidal person made by the general population. The unenlightened see it as a cop-out, an attempt to get attention, or to punish someone. Such people might even give you a gun and tell you to get on with it, thinking to call your bluff. Among those closer to you, you will encounter a great deal of anger from surprising quarters. After my attempt, one of my best friends was furious with me and wanted to tell my husband to dump me. My husband himself told me he would leave if I tried it again because, as he said, "I can't stand it." I think the basis of this kind of behavior is fear — fear of how they would have felt had you succeeded. The prospect is so awful to them that they lash out at you, the perceived cause of their discomfort, without wondering what kind of hell led you to try in the first place. So, in addition to feeling physically and mentally awful you have to endure the censure of your family and friends, and lectures about how they feel. They may ask you such questions as, "How could you do this to us? You have a home, a family, enough money etc. etc... ". Fine. All these things may be perfectly true, but they are also totally irrelevant. You have an illness. They wouldn't blame you for dying of cancer, but if you almost die of a mental illness they will remonstrate forever. Some of them may never be able to forgive you, and this is the time when you need their love most. Of course there are exceptions. My father suffered from depression all his life, but never received help. He did not in

41

the least admonish me — he had entertained such thoughts himself. He understood completely, and said only that he was "infinitely sad" for me.

The hostility I described can even occur in a make-believe situation, which illustrates the power of the concept. I was once involved with training potential leaders of support groups for people with depression. I was to act the part of a suicidal group member so that the students could learn what to do. Although we all knew this was a training practice, one student became absolutely furious with me and stormed out of the room. She epitomized the reaction of outrage that many people have to this idea. Apparently her child had died at a young age some years previously, and she could not forgive me for being alive and "well" and voicing the desire to die. The point is that the person I portrayed is definitely not "well". She was very seriously ill, and in need of immediate help. It makes one wish for some tangible proof of need, such as a great, bleeding hole in the head. We advised the student not to become a support group leader.

You may also encounter some hostility among the non-psychiatric medical staff. For instance, when I attempted to die using cyanide, I was in the Intensive Care Unit (ICU) for about 36 hours. There was one male nurse who was enraged at me. He would do for me what he had to do, but never responded when I thanked him and would not even look at me. Conversely, two psychiatric nurses who had cared for me previously came to the ICU on their lunch break to hold my hands, which were at that point, tied down. The conversation was a bit one-sided because I had three tubes in my mouth at the time, but it was wonderful for me to see them again.

Your physical condition will, of course, depend upon the method you decided to use, your thoroughness, and upon how much time elapsed before someone intervened. Once your physical condition has been stabilized you will swiftly be transferred to a psychiatric unit because other wards are not equipped to handle a suicidal person. Ill as you may be, you might still have the strength to drag yourself over to a window and jump, or find something sharp to injure yourself with.

When you arrive on the psychiatric ward you will automatically be placed on the lowest level of privilege and watched constantly. Kind as the staff may be, they simply cannot afford to trust you, and because you actually made the attempt it will take you longer than usual to earn privileges. A person who has failed an attempt at suicide is much more at risk of trying again than someone who found help during the planning stage. They will watch you like hawks, so do not expect any privacy for a while, but if you are lucky and co-operative you will find them at least supportive and, I hope, kind. You will find that you have virtually no possessions with you, and if your physical condition was critical when you were found, your clothes will have been slit at the sleeves for swift removal. So when you are able to get up you will have no things to wear. Being under such strict supervision will isolate you from the other consumers who, as I have mentioned, could be a valuable source of support. The staff are accustomed to the idea of suicide — it is part of their job. They do understand, but at this point you may not be able to believe that.

It will probably be a relief when you are finally allowed to mingle with the other consumers. You may find that your reputation has preceded you, and they may ask, "Are you the one that...?" You will find that the other consumers display interesting attitudes toward suicide. The veterans will tell you of their previous adventures and joke about how ceiling fans came crashing down on them during abortive attempts to hang themselves. Various methods will be discussed and compared and the method you chose will be assessed as to its effectiveness, and what it says about you. I was regarded with some degree of awe in that I had, a) access to, and b) the nerve to use, cyanide. The general population would be horrified to overhear these discussions. The point is that the seriously mentally ill person **lives with** thoughts of suicide, and how to achieve it, even when he or she is not actively suicidal. I can remember searching out and appropriating things with which to injure or kill myself even when I was supposedly well. I had several caches of cyanide hidden around our apartment which my poor husband, bless him, had to seek out and destroy before I was allowed any privileges. I found these discussions about the practical aspects of suicide very therapeutic, lurid as they may seem. They had the effect of demystifying the act and illustrating what a pointless, unnecessary and pathetic way it is for a human being to die.

So let us consider now your attitude toward yourself. Do you feel ashamed, proud, guilty or sorry that you tried? Do you regard your survival as a failure, or as a piece of good luck? Your attitude toward your action will be closely monitored, and you will find that the staff will return to the subject at every opportunity. You will not even gain any substantial privileges until they are sure that you want to live, at least enough to alert them if you feel suicidal. As I have stated before, total honesty is the only way to a full recovery, even though this may be regarded as silly by some of the other consumers. If you regret that you did not die then you are still in danger. Do not lie to the staff about this, tempting as those privileges may be. The staff are not only trying to help you, they are also trying to protect your loved ones from the trail of emotional havoc that your suicide would leave. Most people try to die because the pain of their illness is intolerable and they cannot believe this will change. They do not want to be dead, only free of pain, which is a perfectly reasonable thing to want. The danger lies in the insidious belief which afflicts most consumers, that nothing can ever change. Because of the stigma that mental illness carries in our society, we tend not to hear about all those who get sick, are helped, and return to the community to lead normal lives. This news might be of help to the potential suicide, although most believe that such a miracle could not be possible for him or her. Some people attempt suicide because their hallucinations tell them to. My own reason was that I was convinced that everyone would, despite their protests to the contrary, be better off, and would actually heave a sigh of relief when I had gone. My suicide would be an act of altruism. Such grandiosity! As if I could ever be that important! There was also a strong desire to be free of the feeling that I was a liability, so I, too, wanted to be free of my particular brand of pain. To the person who is ill, suicide seems a legitimate and reasonable action. I can remember thinking, and I have heard others say this as well, that if my family truly loved me, they would let me go. This is the most dangerous aspect of suicide. This person has long ago shed the horror and repugnance with which it is seen in our society. For the potential suicide the brakes have failed, and, unless helped, he or she will career into the abyss which results in an attempt or in death. So all attempts, even those not regarded as "serious" by emergency room staff, are statements of need. They must be taken seriously, and especially not treated with contempt, either by the public, or the family.

This leads me into a brief discussion of the ethical side of this. There is a distinct difference in the way people react to death from a physical illness and death from a mental illness. Although cancer was once stigmatized, these days, no one would blame you for dying of it. The point is that the cancer, and not you, would be seen as the enemy, and everyone could feel comfortably united in being angry with it. However, people seem unable to see a mental illness as a separate entity from you, the person. So you, instead of your illness, become the target for their quite legitimate anger. In all fairness, your family must be given some consideration here. Because of the way that mental illness is currently perceived in our society, your attempt to die may be seen as a direct reflection of their treatment of you. Consequently, they feel guilty over what you have done, and may feel as though they are being blamed for it by others. They would not have felt guilty had you died of cancer. Sad, yes, but not to blame. So, had you actually died in your attempt, those left behind would have suffered an emotional devastation which could have lasted for the rest of their lives. Now that I have finally recognized the truth of this, I use it as my most potent weapon against thoughts of trying again.

In the last ten years, neuroscientists and geneticists have accumulated powerful volumes of evidence to support the fact that mental illness has a biochemical and genetic basis. Therefore a mental illness is as physical a condition as any other illness, and should be seen as such. It, the illness, is separate from you, the person. Mental illness <u>does</u> change your behavior, but so does physical pain. If you have attempted suicide, your family is perfectly justified in being hurt and angry — but not at <u>you</u>. Their anger should be directed against the disease, and the fact that the treatments we have are so long-winded and uncomfortable. With this in mind, the family would be relieved of their burden of guilt: this would defuse their hostility and everyone would be less miserable.

B. Delirium and Psychosis

A dear friend of mine, who happens also to be an editor, expressed concern at the inclusion of the following description of delirium, because she thought that it would "scare the bejeezus out of some poor newly hospitalized person." It is not intended to do that, but I can see her point. Delirium is terrifying but I describe my experience of it so fully because I want the person in pain to know that even the most bizarre episodes are treatable. People do recover. Of course, it takes time and care and endurance, but here I am, well enough to write this book. I hope also that it may help those who care about you to understand what you are going through. If you do read this, either before or after the episode, then it may help to know that you are not traveling in uncharted territory; others have been there before you, and returned to tell the tale. For a most vivid description of schizophrenic deterioration, I would refer you to the excellent book, <u>The Eden Express.</u> [12] by Mark Vonnigut. My own brief experience of delirium was, thankfully, pallid by comparison.

I am very hazy as to some of the details, such as how long it lasted. I think it was somewhere between one and three days. I was hospitalized at the time, being treated for depression with desipramine, and with unilateral ECT. I was not responding to this regimen, so, to help me further, bilateral ECT was used. I have two recollections of realizing that the staff thought something was wrong, but I am unclear as to which came first. One was an interview with my doctor, a young resident, of whom I politely inquired whether he was aware that my father's grape-vine was growing under his chair. The other was at night. I have no idea as to which night. Apparently, I was found wandering the halls naked. I do remember not having any clothes on, but I could not understand why this caused so much concern. The psychiatric wing of the hospital I was in had a general alarm system, by which the staff could summon help from all the other wards, in an emergency. They told me later that I set off this system twice during that night, but I do not remember that. What I do recall is wondering why everything seemed so weird. Why were the walls breathing? Why was I covered in black jelly-fish that smelt like old running shoes — and why the hell were the staff not aware of all this? I was politely brought up in middle-class Britain, so I resisted the urge to scream and thrash about as long as I could. Once, however, one of them told me that she was unable to help me get the black things off because she did not see them, then something seemed to slip away. My next recollection is of lying on a mattress on the floor of a small bare room which I realized was the seclusion room. A young doctor with a southern accent was holding my arms down, to keep me from breaking my wrists against the wall. They did not use any other form of physical restraint. When I realized that I was in seclusion it made me feel safe, perhaps because they did not close the door, and never left me unattended. One part of me dimly realized that this was where I needed to be. They thought that the high level of medication I had been taking, combined with the bilateral ECT had caused this problem. Consequently, they could not give me any medication to alleviate my symptoms. All they could do was stay with me, encourage me to drink as much fluid as possible and wait. I do not know how long it took. I do remember a sense of unremitting horror at the fact of existence. The walls, the floor, the mattress, all were filled with terror for me. Most of the time the nurse or orderly would sit in the doorway to the room and read, provided I was not making too much fuss. There was, however, one outstanding exception to this. She was a nurse called Patricia, who had a reputation for being very strict. The people with eating disorders called her "Attila the Hun". For some reason, she was assigned to take care of me for part of one night. I was a little bit afraid of her, although nothing she could have done would have been worse than those stinking jelly-fish. But she did not just sit in the doorway, she came right into the room with me, sat on the mattress and took me in her arms. She sang songs to me as though I were a baby. She called the orderly and made him bring her a bowl of ice and some wash-cloths, so that she could put cold packs on my face and neck. I remember thinking, "How can she stand being near me, these things smell so bad?". She stroked my hair, which was damp and greasy, and rocked me until I fell asleep. When I woke up she was gone, her shift had ended, and someone was sitting in the doorway again. I was so sad. I was alone again. What was so important about what she did was that she broke down the terrible isolation I was in. She came right into hell with me and even though she could not see and smell the things that I was seeing and smelling, she did not allow me to be alone. I shall never forget her, and I hope if she reads this she will recognize herself, and my gratitude.

Later, I remember waking to find that my black companions were gone, the walls kept still, and that I was happy. I was exceedingly, terrifyingly happy. This, I was told, was "hypomania", and it lasted about a week. I did not care what they called it, it felt wonderful. The only trouble was that I could not sleep worth a damn, could not eat, could not stop talking and could not keep still. The staff seemed very pleased with my progress. I was still on one-to-one with a nurse, but they all seemed eager to do nice things for me. They took me for walks, one gave me a manicure — everyone seemed delighted that I had weathered the storm.

There are two things that I brought away from that experience. The first was the realization that seclusion in those circumstances was a kindness. It was not a punitive measure taken because I had caused so much trouble with the alarm system. Its purpose was to cut down sensory stimulation, to deprive my brain of more things to generate horrors out of, hence the bare walls and the dim lighting. The second thing I came away with was a sense of amazement at what the human brain can do to itself. My brain had conjured up, and synchronized, three separate sets of sensory hallucination. I could see those jelly-fish, but I could also feel them and smell them. Incredible. This was really something compared to the mere auditory hallucinations to which I was accustomed. Years later, a friend told me that if I had ever tried the hallucinatory drugs that were so popular in the '60s I would not have been so amazed, but being a well brought up little English girl, such things were beyond my ken. Personally, no one could persuade me to try a street-drug after that experience. There is absolutely nothing so precious as a normally functioning brain.

· 4 ·
Now You Are a Mental Case

This chapter has a rather brutal title. That is quite deliberate — unfortunately, you may have some brutal experiences ahead of you. You have just received the most stunning piece of news in your life. Some doctor has decided that you are mentally ill. In fact he or she thinks that you are so crazy that you have to be locked away, at least figuratively, even if you entered the hospital voluntarily. There should, in an ideal world, not be any need for this chapter. The diagnosis of a mental illness should not be any more unfortunate than the diagnosis of diabetes. In our society, however, the diagnosis of any mental illness carries with it a stigma. An article in the Times of London [13] once stated that:

> "[in] a brief public opinion survey of attitudes to mental illness, one third of the sample endorsed the statement that the mentally ill were likely to be violent, and murderers insane."

I must confess that I was pleasantly surprised to read that only one third of the population perceive us as violent. So, this is what the mentally ill have to face. After your diagnosis there is a new need for acceptance of you, which was not there before. This chapter is about acceptance and rejection: how to achieve the first and side-step the second.

A. Your Attitudes Toward Yourself
When I was diagnosed, I remember thinking that this could not really be happening . Mental illness is like that car crash that can never happen to you — until it does. After my diagnosis I went through several phases; self-rejection, followed by "acceptance-with-apology", followed, much later, by "acceptance-with-defiance". Now I have "acceptance-with-gratitude".

As the first person in my family ever to be diagnosed as mentally ill, I rejected myself as though I had done something foul on the carpet. Not only did I blame myself, but I also thought of myself as a malingerer. Although I knew that I was telling the doctors the truth, I could not believe myself. I knew that I did hear a Voice telling me to kill myself, I knew that I heard screams in my head, but these symptoms seemed too fantastic to be real. I thought that I must be generating them in some way so as to get attention, or to have an excuse for being such a worthless creature in the first place. For many years, during my bleaker periods, I asked my doctor whether I was really ill, or whether in fact I was "making it up". He patiently reassured me every time. Only through the unquestioning and enduring acceptance of the professionals, could I accept myself as a person with a problem. To have something biochemically wrong with your brain does not mean that you are not still a <u>person</u>. To accept yourself fully you have to believe in this fact. This is not easy, and the task took me years to achieve.

I know that my gradual self-acceptance resulted in the second phase of my reaction to the diagnosis. I started to think of myself as a walking problem — not for myself, but for others. In my work as a research technician, I became more than ever prone to the belief that if something went wrong with an experiment, it must have been my fault. This led to my being doubtful and guilt-ridden every single working day. I made myself be extra thorough and I worked very long hours in order to compensate for my being, as I saw it, impaired. I was constantly checking up on myself, and asking if I were doing a good enough job. Apparently, I was, because I was allowed to keep my position even after repeated and lengthy periods in the hospital, and one suicide attempt. Whenever my pay check arrived I felt guilty — I had not earned this, I must have conned them into thinking that I deserved this money. This attitude of apology — not only for my illness, but for my existence — indicated two things; first, that I had not fully accepted myself, and second, that my depression still was not adequately controlled. Luckily for me, I had a therapist who seemed not only willing but eager to see me. I kept on pestering him with questions as to whether I really should be taking up his time. I tried hard to convince him that I was not worth all this effort. Of course, had he agreed with me I would have been devastated, but I felt obliged, out of a sense of justice and fairness to him, to give him every opportunity to ditch me. I even — and we both laugh over this now — tried to take up as little space as possible, by jamming myself into one corner of his sofa, to the extent that I wore a little hole in it at that place. To my great good fortune, however, he insisted that I continue to see him and, as the months and years went by, I gradually came to the point of finding myself more acceptable, for more of the time. I sometimes think that after compassion and empathy, plain old-fashioned pig-headedness is the quality that a good therapist needs most.

The impact of your diagnosis, will be especially urgent to you if you have children. It may seem to pose a huge threat to their early childhood. If they are older, you must wonder what sort of role-model you are, and this concern may become so intense as to impede your recovery. Consumers have described to me their massive sense of guilt after their diagnosis, and their urgent desire that it not impinge upon their children. Some prefer not to tell their children anything, out of the understandable desire not to hurt them. Some need to retain a sense of control, and may demand higher standards of behavior than was usual before the diagnosis. I will not presume to offer any suggestions on this, as I have no children. As always, I would recommend talking to other consumers who are also parents.

There was also the issue of taking medication, although this was more easily dealt with. At first it seemed to be a disgrace for me to be reliant upon any sort of "crutch". But as I saw that the medication actually did help, I realized two things. The first was that if a chemical could help me, then the problem must have at least some basis in biochemistry, and that made it somehow less "my fault". The second thing I realized was that if I felt better and less guilty, I was more useful and had more energy to give, both to my husband and to my employers. So to my convoluted mind taking medication became less of a crutch, and more of a duty. I could handle duty.

As you become more able to accept yourself fully — no small achievement — you will find that you are more easily accepted by others. You will start to believe that you have as much right to be treated decently, as does any other human being. Once you truly believe that, your behavior will change in subtle ways. These changes will convey that you expect to be treated as a human being and do not accept being patronized or ignored. As this occurred in me, I stopped being furtive and apologetic about my illness, and became completely open about it. I always made a point of telling any potential employer about the problem at my first interview, so that no accusations of deception could be leveled at me later. I was almost defiant about it, challenging people with the knowledge of my problem, daring them to show themselves up as ignorant or judgmental. The rationale behind this was that I thought, "If this person has a problem with my history, then I want to know about it now." I also felt — and do still feel — that to be secretive about the problem only perpetuates its stigma. Why should there be any grounds for accusations of deceit if a person does not reveal a mental illness at an interview? My form of protest against this was as follows: if I could be seen to be an adequate, worthwhile person in the work-place, in spite of my mental illness, then perhaps I could change the attitudes of my colleagues toward those of the mentally ill not fortunate enough to be able to work. Now my form of protest is more direct — I am writing this book.

B. The Attitudes of Others Toward You

The acceptance of your parents and relations may also be hard to achieve, because you are, at least in part, a product of their upbringing, so they may think that your diagnosis reflects badly on them. I was living in America at the time of my diagnosis, and my mother's first response to the news was, "Well, why don't you come home? You were never depressed here." It was easy and convenient for her to blame the USA She saw my illness as something that someone should be blamed for, and it was not going to be her! Her reaction was not so very different from my own.

You will also encounter rejection outside your immediate family. I am always concerned as to whether this is real, or whether I perceive it because I expect to. I think that sometimes I have perceived prejudice because I was expecting it, but not always. As with the psychiatric professionals, some people are enlightened, and some are not. A lack of prejudice is not necessarily associated with a college education, and those whom you have decided to trust can surprise you with their ignorance at times. Some time later, at a different job, the Voice was bothering me so I completed my work and went home. The next day I was admonished for this, and warned not to do it again. I pointed out that one of my colleagues had recently gone home during the day, with a physical ailment. I was told, "Yes, but she had a legitimate reason." Someone in the higher echelons regarded self-destructive hallucinations merely as a convenient excuse to leave early. Is hearing a Voice berating you, and telling you to injure yourself, any less painful than the gall-bladder attack that had caused my colleague's departure?

It is an unfortunate fact, but you will also encounter such ignorance within the medical profession. An oral surgeon I was once referred to treated me like a retarded four-year-old after I told him that I was on psychoactive medication. He flatly refused to answer my questions about the surgery he was to perform on my jaw, responding only with the statement, "That is not an issue for you."

These are just a few of the experiences that have resulted from others knowing of my diagnosis. I have heard far worse stories. I hope yours will not be one of them.

At the start of this chapter I foolishly stated that I would offer some pearls of wisdom on how to achieve acceptance and avoid rejection. Well, there are not many pearls, but here goes. In order to achieve respect, you must show that, in spite of your pain, you respect yourself — even when you do not. Sometimes you just have to fake it. There are practical things that you can do, which, however pointless they may seem at the time, can help you to feel more in control.

As far as you are able, whether you are in, or out, of the hospital, keep your living area as clean and neat as possible. Similarly, keep your clothes and person as clean as you can, and pay attention to your appearance. Remember, you are a person, you deserve respect, and you are more likely to get it if you seem to be in control. These activities can be a way of fighting. They convey, both to you, and to others, that although you have some horrendous problems, you are not going to let them control you. When I am ill, my house is cleaner, and I am better dressed, than when I am well. It is part of my arsenal. My husband becomes concerned when the house is spotless; but if he can see some dog-hair, and I am sitting on the floor engrossed in a book, then he knows that all is well.

There are other things that you can do. Organize yourself. Many consumers, myself included, have trouble concentrating, and remembering things. Keep a small diary with you always, and write down everything. Be punctual for your appointments. Allow plenty of time for traveling, because public transport is unpredictable. If you keep on trying to do these things, even when you are feeling awful, I guarantee that you will increase your self-respect, and will be more readily accepted by others. This regimen will also help you to avoid rejection, although this is a more difficult issue because, while you can control the way that you present yourself, you cannot control the years of prejudice that may be entrenched in the person you are dealing with. Much as I have advocated honesty as a means of battling stigma, it is wise to be cautious sometimes. If you sense that someone is going to hurt you — and you will become extremely good at this — then either avoid that person, or at least let him or her get to know you, as a person, before you reveal any problems. You will also find yourself choosing friends who will not hurt you, and avoiding those situations that cause stress and worsen your symptoms.

It is now sixteen years since the time of my original diagnosis. I still feel like an ambassador for the mentally ill. I still feel that I have to do things extra well to compensate for my inadequacies. I also feel that I must think more clearly, if I can, before stating any opinions, lest I be thought of as "flaky". In other words I am still reacting to my diagnosis and probably will continue to do so for the rest of my life. I have already stated that one of the most important and difficult things that you have to do after your diagnosis, is to achieve self-acceptance. I am repeatedly outraged at the many thoughtless ways in which our benighted society makes this task more difficult. In most people, self-acceptance is deeply integrated with their experience of acceptance from others. The mentally ill suffer extra needless pain because of the way in which their problems are dealt with by the so-called mentally well.

C. Your Attitudes Toward Other Consumers

I have found that, since my diagnosis, and especially after my first time in the hospital, I have become deeply sympathetic toward the mentally ill. To my shame, before my diagnosis, I never even thought about them. Why should I? They had nothing to do with me; as I sailed along in my yuppie little life. But now I think about the mentally ill every day. Often, at eight a.m. I think about the hospitalized anorexics who are in the same time-zone as I, facing the first meal of their food-laden day. On weekends and holidays, I think of those in the hospital who have no outside privileges, especially if the weather is fine. On the street, if I see someone talking to himself, I wonder whether there is anything I can, or should, do. If you see someone having a heart attack, you call an ambulance. Why should the course of action be so unclear when someone is obviously hallucinating? Such people are usually avoided, because their behavior is alarming. I attribute my increased sensitivity as a reflection of less fear.

Once, when I was walking into the psychiatric institute where my husband works, a middle-aged man approached me. "Would you please buy me some shampoo?" he asked gently. I knew exactly where he was coming from. He had earned enough privileges to leave the building, but not enough to leave the hospital grounds. Consequently, if he crossed the road to the convenience store, he might jeopardize those hard-earned privileges and again be confined to the building. "Certainly," I replied, getting out my money. "No, no." he protested, pressing a $20 bill into my hands. The poor soul was prepared to trust a total stranger with what was probably all the money he had at that time. So, I took his money, bought him the largest bottle of shampoo in the store, and returned with it, the change, and the receipt, to where he stood waiting. He thanked me profusely, clutching the bottle to his chest. Before my problems surfaced I would probably have avoided him. So you could say that I have developed a sense of affinity with the mentally ill, and I sincerely hope that I never lose it. As I have said before, some of the kindest, and brightest people I have ever met have been consumers.

During my various periods in the hospital, I have met consumers who were also medical doctors, a nurse, a social worker, a stockbroker, a lumberjack and a university professor of Russian literature who spoke five other languages. Mental illness does not confine itself to the poor and uneducated. We are all at risk. Many consumers are poor and appear to be to be uneducated, but this is only because their illness prevents them from realizing their full potential. If you cannot concentrate because of voices in your head, then you are less likely to keep your job, then you cannot pay the mortgage or the rent, and so the downward spiral starts. So much is lost to our society through these most horrible forms of illness.

D. Your Attitudes Toward the "Normal" World

Since my illness, I have noticed a lot more "craziness" in the normal world than I ever did before. For instance, since my bout of delirium I simply cannot comprehend why anyone should wish to take a hallucinatory drug, which is bound to impair their functioning brain. When there are so many fascinating things to read and learn and do in this world, why waste good brain-time on illusions? I have had my share of times when my brain was not functioning, and I really appreciate the times when it does. Why put that in jeopardy?

I have found myself becoming increasingly sensitive to the use of psychiatric terminology in general parlance, for example the term "suicide" used to describe the degree of spiciness of Buffalo Wings. This can be very upsetting, especially when you have only recently left the hospital. Jokes about mental illness can also be very hurtful, and feel as though they are being aimed especially at you. All I can suggest is that you keep in mind that many people do not understand, and that other forms of misfortune are also the subject of jokes. Remember, if you can, that you are no less a person because of your particular type of pain. I will have more to say about this in my concluding chapters.

I have a dear friend who is a recovered anorexic. She tells me of how infuriated she feels about the preoccupation that our society has with weight, diet, and calories. This was not something I had noticed before knowing her, and it is another example of our indifference toward the pain of mental illness.

Sometimes I come across people who ask me about the "positive aspects" of mental illness. I always wonder if they would address the same question to a quadriplegic or to someone who had leukemia. I find it slightly insulting. Any incapacitating illness is a waste of life. I have sometimes spent hours on the floor, howling, because the screams in my head were overwhelming. That time can never be had again. The months that I have spent in the hospital were not only unproductive, but very expensive. As far as I can see, there are almost no positive aspects to mental illness, except those that result from its remission. The relief of symptoms brings with it exuberance, because one is back in reality. Leaving the hospital brings great joy. Every single normal day that I have, I am grateful for. I pause in wonder at people who become genuinely upset at the unsightliness of their neighbor's garden, or the inefficacy of their laundry detergent. If you are well, there is so much more to life. These, however, are gifts that would inevitably follow any prolonged traumatic experience. I recall that my father said something very similar after World War II.

There is much in the current media which suggests that creativity is genetically linked to madness. Most of this is anecdotal, which I find distasteful, probably because of my scientific training. I have, found, however, two properly controlled studies in which this hypothesis is supported[14; 15]. I feel very uneasy about this, because it seems to imply that the mentally ill should atone for their illness by being creative. If someone with a mental illness happens also to be creative, then that is great, but there should be no suggested requirement or expectation of this. As for the idea that mental illness actually enhances creativity, all I can say is that I cannot write when I am depressed — there is too much pain, and my writing seems worthless to me, and therefore pointless.

Finally, I have to say that my illness has resulted in an increase both in my cynicism, and my compassion — odd companions, I suppose. In the struggle to be well I have had to take apart, examine, and reassemble almost every aspect of my life. I am a much more humble person than I was, but also more assured. These things are very good, but they are dearly bought. One thing is sure — the experience of mental illness will leave you forever changed. You will never be the same again. All you can do is to try to make these inevitable changes as positive as possible.

· 5 ·
Getting Better

This is a delightful chapter for me to write. It will cover the remainder of your hospitalization and your discharge. I have been looking forward to this. So far, most of the things I have been telling you to expect have been unpleasant, because I thought that if you were prepared for them, they might be less awful for you. Now I can tell you about the wonderful, and surprising aspect of a psychiatric hospitalization — you can get better! This prospect seems unbelievable when you are in pain, but it can happen, and does.

Those who recover best are the ones we do not hear from, because they are quietly getting on with their lives. However, in the harsh nineties, "getting better" is much more complicated than it used to be. Does it mean that your problems are over, and you can return to normal life? Maybe. Or does it mean that you are moving on to another set of problems? Probably. I have decided to restructure this chapter into two sections. The first will cater to those who are well enough to cope when they are discharged, and have something to return to. The second section will attempt to address the predicament of those who are still in pain at discharge, and have only minimal support in the community.

If you are still hospitalized when you start to recover, you are not likely to be the first person to notice any change in your condition. The staff, who are used to observing patients, may notice slight differences in you, even while you still think it is impossible for you to be well. The other consumers, who are also acutely perceptive, may also be among the first to notice change. This has happened to me, and I have found it intensely irritating to be told that I was "doing better" when I, in fact, still thought I felt awful. Not only is it annoying to be told how you feel, but it can also cause guilt for not feeling better when you are "supposed to". So you might feel very alone. With this in mind, when I think I see an improvement in anyone, I tell him or her so, but also ask if it is real. This avoids imposing my viewpoint on the person, who may actually still be in need of support.

Recovery from a mental illness is strange, and wonderful. I can only draw from the experience of recovery from depression, but I am not unique — there are features that are common to recovery from most types of mental illness. The essence of recovery is that you are returned to reality. Reality is a very comforting thing, as compared to the horrors to which the human brain can subject itself. You are no longer isolated in that awful, desolate place that is your illness. This manifests itself in strange and subtle ways, quite separate from merely the cessation of your most distressing symptoms. One of the joys of recovery has often been for me, that my body feels better. Not only do I have more energy, but I feel as though I am better coordinated, can move more freely, and am less clumsy. I know that my posture improves, and I can accomplish simple tasks more efficiently. I also had the sensation that I had physically returned from another place, as from a journey. There was also the feeling that I could see and hear better, and colors seemed very bright. This is not so very surprising, considering that psychiatric illnesses cause such enormous preoccupation with inner pain and/or hallucinations. When this preoccupation is relieved, you have more energy to devote to what is going on around you. You may start to feel bored. Boredom is a good sign, it means that you can see how unstimulating a psychiatric ward is designed to be.

At this stage you may find yourself noticing the others' behavior, making allowances for their pain, and helping them in ways that were once helpful to you. You may, surprisingly, find yourself among the "veterans" of the ward. You may even find yourself to be one of those creatures who can actually laugh, and you will recall how impossible this seemed to you on your first day. Simple things, such as taking a shower, will seem less burdensome, and may become pleasurable to you. Both male and female consumers sometimes take more interest in their appearance, and even if the changes are small, you may be asked, "Have you changed your hair ?" People see a difference, but cannot quite be sure of what it is.

As your recovery proceeds, you will start to receive more privileges. This is very exciting, after the confinement you have been experiencing, even if it is only that you are no longer under close observation. Eventually, you will be allowed to leave the ward and you will find yourself wandering around the hospital as though it were Aladdin's cave. Everything will be fascinating and delightful to you. Of course the really big step is to be allowed your first "pass". This means that you can leave the hospital for a predetermined block of time. The other consumers will congratulate you, as though you were graduating. The staff will want you to plan what you are going to do, and with whom, and they may even want you to achieve a certain goal. A pass is not just a holiday, although that is how it feels; it is part of the treatment plan, and an experiment to see how well you can cope "outside". You will count the hours until your pass commences, and it will come, and you will go out of the building for the first time!

It may come as a surprise to find that your pass, much as you relished it, is not altogether enjoyable. You may be unexpectedly scared. I have felt very conspicuous in the street at these times, as though I were physically distorted. Also I have found the city traffic terrifying, even as a pedestrian. There may be a feeling of "sensory overload" especially if you go into a large and busy shopping mall. It is wise not to be too ambitious on your first pass. Do not spend the time alone if you can possibly avoid it, and unless you are really feeling well, do not drive. There is just so much more information to process outside than in the hospital, which is precisely why you needed to be there in the first place. Remember, also, that after weeks of inactivity in the hospital your body is debilitated and you will rapidly become tired. If you become agitated, or your symptoms start to reappear, you always have the option of returning from your pass early. This may seem like sacrilege after you have been confined for so long, and going back into the hospital building is a most crushing experience. Bear in mind also, that once you go back, you cannot change your mind and leave again — your pass is over. If you do need to return early from your pass, your family or friends may not understand this, and may feel insulted. This will add to your stress, and is another good reason to plan your pass with care. Passes are only allowed for set periods of time. One aspect of your pass that is unavoidably distressing is the knowledge that, like Cinderella, you have to go back at a certain time. If you reliably return from your pass at the correct time, you will be trusted to have another, perhaps longer pass. So, awful as it feels to go back — and it does feel awful — do return on time — and start immediately to plan for the next one! After you have returned, a nurse will talk with you to find out what you did, where you went, and how you responded to the circumstances. This information will be noted in your chart, and used to assess your progress.

Now that you are recovering, you will find that your relationships with the other consumers will change. If you are lucky, you will find yourself being supportive, rather than supported, for more of the time. You will, I hope, have formed some strong friendships among the others. You may also find new friends among those who, previously hostile or withdrawn, are also starting to recover. As a psychosis clears in one of your colleagues, you may feel as though you are meeting a whole new person, unknown to you before, even though you have lived in close proximity for several weeks.

There is an ethical dilemma that you might run into during your recovery, caused by your new alertness and your closeness to the other consumers. You will be privy to their secrets. If these secrets include self-destructive behavior, you may be torn between respect for your friend's privacy, and concern for his or her welfare and recovery. You might suggest to your friend that he or she tell the staff about this behavior. This can sometimes work out very well, because a discussion of the problem with staff may help your friend to transcend the need for the behavior in question, and can actually result in real progress. If the person does not agree to this, then, unless the situation is life-threatening, there is not much else you can do. This problem should not occur if the staff are alert and observant.

Your relationships with the staff will also change, as you recover. You may find yourself sharing jokes and teasing them, or feeling especially drawn towards the few who have been especially helpful and empathetic. As you approach discharge you may find yourself feeling very scared and lost at the prospect of leaving them. This anxiety may cause a slight relapse, about which you might feel a furtive kind of relief — if you are sick again they will not make you leave so soon, right? Do not worry, the staff will be expecting this as soon as discharge is mentioned. I am in no way implying that you are malingering. The return of your symptoms is real enough —

leaving the hospital is a scary business, and that stress can cause your symptoms to return. It is quite natural.

I would like to discuss briefly your feelings of gratitude and affection toward those of the staff who have helped you. I always felt that there was no way in which I could ever thank these people enough, after they had restored to me my life. You may want to give them things, expensive things if you can afford them, because being well feels so marvelous. Remember that they have professional guidelines as to what they can, and cannot, accept from patients, and that by surprising them with lavish gifts, you are putting them in a very difficult position. They may not want to refuse the things you bring, aware as they are that you may feel rejected, but they simply cannot accept large gifts. So, to avoid putting them in this situation, keep your offerings small and impersonal, such as chocolates or flowers, or something that can be shared by the whole ward. Conversely, you are not at all obliged to give them anything, so do not feel that you are. Your courtesy, friendship, and recovery will amply reward them. One word of caution. You may have intense feelings of gratitude and affection toward your doctor after what has been done for you. These feelings are a natural part of the therapeutic process, and are in no way wrong. If, however, you attempt to demonstrate them physically, as in a hug, you may be surprised at how fast your doctor can leap through the nearest aperture in an attempt to preserve his or her hard-earned license. Unfortunately, these days, there are very strict guidelines set down by the medical associations about physical contact between doctor and patient. To avoid this embarrassing situation, you will have to pack as much feeling as you can into words, and a formal handshake.

So, you finally have a discharge date. You will have had several passes by now, and have enjoyed them more and more. It has been decided that you will be able cope "outside". This is very exciting, and the last few days of your stay will seem interminable. At this point, a social worker will discuss with you the living situation that you will return to. There may be aspects of your life that need to be changed, so that you do not get sick again. When I was leaving the hospital for the ninth time, the candid young doctor in charge of my case, said to me, "You've been in hospital nine times in eleven years. Doesn't that tell you something?" After all my previous hospitalizations, I had returned to the research lab, to do work which, as I have mentioned, filled me with guilt and misgiving. Appalling as it then seemed, I realized that I had to do something else or remain chronically depressed, and useless to everybody. I am not suggesting that by changing your job or your living situation, you will be forever well. As I have said, I am a firm believer in the biochemical basis of mental illness. Stress, however, will make your symptoms worse, and right now you need all the help you can get. It is your social worker's job to examine with you, all aspects of your life, and produce some sort of plan of adjustments that will keep you as well as is possible. If you were so mentally ill as to have needed hospitalization, that means you were pretty sick — in this economic climate people are not hospitalized for minor problems. Had you been physically ill to an equivalent degree, no one would expect you to be totally well at the time of your discharge, so it is essential that some sort of "safety net" be set up for you. Your family could still find your illness hard to understand — they may want to sweep the whole episode under the carpet, and object to any form of continuing care. As you are particularly vulnerable at this time, you could find it hard to oppose them — well meaning relatives can be the source of much pain for you. If this is a problem, tell your social worker, and a "family meeting" can be arranged, in which the needs, both of you, and of your family, are addressed. This may help — and it may not, people can be very intransigent over these issues. Opposing your family may seem difficult, or even criminal to you. It will take a lot of courage on your part, but it is better than getting sick again.

Discharge day has arrived. You will have packed, said your good-byes to your friends among the staff and consumers, swapped telephone numbers, and made promises to keep in touch. Your discharge papers and prescriptions are ready at the nursing station. Without these you cannot leave, so it is a good idea to remind your nurse about them as early as you can. You are anxiously awaiting transport to wherever you are going. As you leave the hospital building, and for the rest of that day, do not feel surprised or guilty if you find yourself experiencing some regrets. It is a natural reaction to leaving a place where you have come to feel safe. You may be very scared at the prospect of having to cope with life, in the real world. You may be very afraid that your illness will come back, in spite of all those contingency plans you made with your social worker. If you are going into a different living situation than you had before, that in itself is frightening. Even if you are going back to a loving family, you may still feel a little "homesick" for the ward. At least there you were never alone, and you did not have to look normal. I can remember being appalled at the prospect of having to structure my own time, decide what to eat, what to do, and where to do it, in spite of the fact that I had been fretting at the hospital restrictions before I left. You may also sense the expectations that your family may have of you, and feel that you cannot live up to them. Bizarre as this will seem, you may even feel that you want to return to the ward. All these feelings are quite natural, expect them, and do not feel guilty about having them. Dealing with life after a psychiatric hospitalization can be, quite frankly, terrifying. There are no magic formulae, but I will offer some suggestions in my final chapter.

This leads me into my next section. What happens if your are discharged after a very short time, with symptoms that still bother you, and little or no support? Some of the previous section will have relevance to you, but in a more hurried way — you may not have had time to make friends among the staff, or worry about a fellow-consumer's behavior. You will have to rely heavily on government-run social programs and agencies. These are cash-strapped, and will become more so, which means that finding, and using them takes energy and motivation — things which you may not have in abundance if you are still coping with your symptoms. I have investigated this from a consumer's point of view, and I have a few suggestions which may help you get the best from the system.

Firstly, the help that you need is probably out there somewhere — your biggest difficulty will be in finding it, and getting it to respond to your needs. Rural areas are much less well supplied with all types of health care than are cities, and mental health is no exception. The two biggest pitfalls of this process are keeping all the details straight in your head, and not giving up. You can tackle both of these with a cheap notebook. Dedicate it to the purpose of holding information together for you, and head for your local library. There you can find the names of consumer/survivor advocacy and information resources. The telephone directory should also have similar information. Collect the names of as many of these agencies as you can, and do not assume that because you have not heard about them, they do not exist. Note their names, addresses and phone numbers, their hours of operation, and what they are set up to provide. If you speak to a live person, as opposed to a machine, ask for that person's name so that you can refer to him or her in your future dealings with that agency. Note the date on which you called them and the outcome of each call. Define your specific needs, and try to apply for each at the appropriate agency. If someone tells you they do not provide that service, then ask them who does. They should know — it's their job. Ask them what you need to be eligible for their service — even in these days of "self-referral" they may still require a letter from your doctor. Record all this in your notebook — don't expect yourself to remember all this information. No one could. Agencies come and go — mostly they go — so your records will help you to keep track of who is still in business.

Your notebook can also help with your despair. It is terribly unfair that you should have to deal with all this when you are just out of the hospital, but that is how things are right now in our society. You may well feel overwhelmed. Try, if you can, to make at least one call a day, and <u>record</u> it. Just the fact that you have written evidence of your efforts can help to boost your morale.

When you do find someone who can supply you with what you need, you may still, unfortunately, be put on a waiting list. Try not to see this as a defeat. Being on a waiting list is better than not being on one. If you are persistent, you might be given a case-worker. These people are there to help you through this discouraging process, but they are all overworked. If you have your own record of what you have applied for and where, you can save yourself both time and frustration.

Another difficulty which you will almost certainly encounter is that the various agencies do not talk to each other. One will see you as a body to be housed, another will see you as a bundle of symptoms, while a third regards you only as a mouth to be fed. No one acknowledges the fact that these things are connected in the form of a living person — you. An example would be of the food-bank giving you cheese when you are taking an MAOI antidepressant. Some agencies will try to be mutually exclusive. If you are receiving help from one, then the other may refuse to help you, even though they provide different services.

I discovered these things by spending hours on the phone, making inquiries on behalf of a fictitious "friend" who had just been discharged, and had no supports. It was and overwhelming and depressing experience, and I was only doing it as an academic exercise. At least half the calls led to voice mail. Had I not had my own phone number to leave on their tape, those calls would have gone nowhere. One of the first things you need is a warm dry place with a phone that you can take calls on. Fortunately some community support groups recognize this and will provide them.

Now for the good news! If you live in a large urban area, some of these issues may have been addressed. For instance, in Toronto there is one agency whose sole purpose is to collect all this information. They publish a book [16] which provides much of the information you will need, such as the names of agencies, and what they are set up to provide. It is regularly updated, and is free to consumers in the metro area. There may be some similar project in your town. The discontinuities that occur in mental health care are slowly being recognized, and efforts are under way to "educate the system" so that the professionals in one organization will at least be vaguely aware of what their colleagues elsewhere are trying to do. Large cities tend also to have mobile crisis response teams and outreach programs to care for those consumers who fall through the cracks. Rural areas are not so well endowed.

Having researched and restructured this chapter, I have reached one ironic conclusion — only those who are really mentally well can hope to get the best out of the system as it stands. Anyone who needs what it can provide, and who does not have a Ph.D. in Information Science, is going to be bewildered and frustrated. I do not say it will never change, but that's how it is right now.

· 6 ·
The Rest of Your Life

At Home — or Not

So now you are at "home", wherever that is. If you are fortunate enough to have a home situation that you can return to, this will be a delight to you. Ordinary tasks, or those things that you would usually think of as chores, become interesting, simply because you can do them without asking permission, and <u>no one is watching you.</u> You may even find yourself wandering around your home just touching things, during that first day. Even broken, dirty, or irritating things will seem like old friends. Now that you are recovering, you may find that you have the energy and enthusiasm to plan projects that you could not have contemplated when you were ill.

If, on the other hand, you do not have a home, or you have decided not to go back there, then you will be going into a whole new environment, and this will naturally make you anxious. You are especially vulnerable now — you have so recently been ill. If your previous home situation was considered so destructive that you are not returning to it, then your need for change was desperate. Needless to say, you are in no condition to go on a therapist-hunt when you have just left the hospital, so it is essential that your treatment team set you up with someone <u>before</u> your actual discharge. If, in time, you just do not feel comfortable with this person, then you can go "shopping", but do, at least have someone to call upon in those first few weeks, after leaving the hospital.

The Need for Change

In the last chapter I touched upon the subject of change. Sometimes, as in my case, the need for change is not obvious — or at least not obvious to the one in pain. Consumers, myself included, can be exasperatingly resistant to change because it is so terrifying. Many sane and sensible women frequently return to their abusive husbands, even when everyone who is trying to help them can see that their very lives are in jeopardy. When mentally ill, people often feel that their grasp upon reality is, at best, tenuous. In order to maintain that grasp, bizarre and often destructive environments are tolerated because they are familiar. Consumers resist change because their world is already almost unmanageable. When some total stranger comes along and suggests that they disrupt the only things that they feel they can cling to, of course they are going to resist. A psychiatric nurse once told me that sometimes the mentally ill live as though they were dangling over a huge chasm, clinging only to a slippery strand of spaghetti. A better way of life may be available to them in the form of a thick and knotted rope by which they can climb out of the chasm. The snag is that, in order to reach the rope, they must let go of the spaghetti. Science was my spaghetti strand, and I clung to it, even when I was suicidal. As I have stated, I am a firm believer in the biochemical basis of mental illness. If, however, you return to exactly the same emotional environment that you lived in when you became ill, you are greatly increasing the chances of a relapse. Believe me, I should know — it took eleven years and nine hospitalizations to get that through my skull. Now, giving up those old habits or occupations, and leaping across to that rope is very, very scary. For this you need support. You do not have to rearrange all aspects of your life at once — that would be hazardous to your health, but clearly, changes must be made. With the help of your therapist you have to find out what to change, then you have to give yourself permission to change, then you have actually to do it. I am in the middle of that process — I have not quite reached the rope yet, but, with the generous support of my doctor/friend I am getting there.

Staying Well

Section 1. Develop Your Arsenal

As with any illness, consistent recovery depends in large part upon those contributions that you make to the situation. Let us suppose that the symptoms that took you to the hospital are now controlled to a tolerable extent. You can function well enough to take care of your basic needs. How can you improve on this? What we all have to do at this point is consciously and deliberately to develop a set of activities and a life-style that nurtures recovery and discourages the return of pain. This "arsenal" as I call it, will be useful not only in pragmatic ways, but will also give you a sense of control, and diminish any sense of helplessness that you may have.

Each consumer's arsenal will be unique, tailored specifically to that person's needs, resources, and style of life. There are, however, some weapons that we can all use, and these I will discuss first.

First, there is psychotherapy and medication. Together, these have been the most important weapons in my arsenal. Psychotherapy does not require an MD. It does require trust, and mutual respect, and you must feel safe enough to tell this person anything. If you are taking any psychoactive medication, you will need an MD. to prescribe it. Usually, a psychiatrist is best for this purpose, it being his or her business to keep informed of the latest types of regimen. However, your family physician may be just as good or better, provided he or she is interested in you, and is prepared to refer you for a consultation if you are not progressing. Let your doctor be your ally, and your first line of defense. Let the prescribed medication be your second weapon — always take it as instructed, and always report the results as thoroughly and honestly as you can.

There is another weapon which we can all share. Pay attention to your physical health. I have never been overweight, and so, until I was prodded into it by my therapist, I had never given much thought to the need for exercise. He suggested that I pick one activity that I did not hate too much and do it regularly for at least a month. Being a loner, with not much money, I chose running because I could do it at any time, and all I really needed was a pair of shoes. I started with an $8 pair from Sears, so that I should not feel too guilty if I did not persist. I have to state that I <u>hated</u> it. I must be very pig-headed though, because I did persist, much to my own surprise. The pay-off was that running acted as a tremendous antidepressant. I do not know whether this was due to those endorphins that we hear so much about, or whether it came from a sense of achievement at having conquered my aversion three times a week. As I became more fit, I actually started to enjoy running and at one point was out every day. You do not have to do that — all you have to do is find what works for <u>you</u>. I cannot over-emphasize the benefit of regular exercise. It acts as a wonderful tranquilizer, and other activities, such as hauling out the trash, seem much less of a chore when you are physically fit. I do wholeheartedly recommend that you find whatever form of exercise suits you best, and make it part of your arsenal — it has no adverse side-effects, and you do not need a drug plan!

Along with exercise, of course, goes a sensible diet. The physical problems caused by a bad diet do not appear immediately, and it is hard to worry about them when your chief concern is your mental health. However, your brain is part of your physical body, and it functions best if that body is well. You can obtain information on good nutrition in the library, or from your doctor. Then you can tailor your diet to your own specific needs and budget. It may seem overwhelming, but it need not be much trouble. Set small goals for yourself. Fruit is cheap and needs little preparation. If you usually live on junk, and you replace one meal a day with fresh fruit, you have taken an important step toward a healthy diet.

There is also the question of getting enough sleep. I am very bad at this. When I am well I want to stay up late because I am engrossed in something — like writing this — and when I am ill my sleep is disturbed and I wake up too early. It is a fact, however, that your brain needs regular and sufficient sleep to function normally, and you will undermine your other efforts by not paying attention to this. This is hard if you have noisy neighbors. Earplugs may help until you can change your situation.

Having established these three basics, you can now start to find weapons of your own. Try to identify — maybe with your doctor's help — those aspects of your life that are self-destructive, or that worsen your symptoms. These activities or habits may have been with you for a long time, so changing them will not be easy. At least, if you have identified these behaviors, then you know what you have to try not to do. The rest is up to you. Some activities may be relatively easy to avoid. I have promised both my doctor, and my husband, that I will seek help when I feel the urge to injure myself, so I can now be relied upon to do that, and it has been a long time since I last actually hurt myself. Other things may be much more difficult, such as habits of thought. My particular problem there is that I indulge in guilty, and self-critical thoughts. They seem so very appropriate, and have been with me all my life. They are with me still.

Now we come to the part of your arsenal that is absolutely unique to you. All I can suggest here is that you try, when your symptoms threaten you, to find a variety of non-destructive activities that help you to transcend your pain. I cannot know what will help you. I can tell you what helps me, and you might want to try some of these things. You really have to find your own set of weapons, and this will take time — I am offering the distillate of eleven years of trial and error. One more thing. You will find that what works for you in one situation, may not work in another, so do not abandon an idea because it does not always help. You have to juggle your weapons to fit the circumstances, so keep a list of all those things that have been known to help you. Mental illness is not static, and you will learn, with time, how to respond to the different aspects of your pain.

My problems start with a feeling of general unease, which escalates to anxiety, at which point the screams which I hear begin. Without intervention, this is followed by a conviction that I am a worthless liability, that all that I do is, by definition, of no value, and that all forms of activity are pointless. That is when all I really want to do is to hide under a blanket, immobile, for hours, and have nothing to do with anything. That is absolutely the very worst thing I can do at that time. It would give me the opportunity to listen to the screaming, feel the pain, and sooner or later the Voice would make Herself heard, followed by the urge to injure myself. Somewhere during that downward spiral I have at least to try to take control.

Usually I am so distressed by that time that reading is out, and I try to stay busy with something that is not intellectually demanding. What I do is clean house. The rationale behind this is that, "I may be totally worthless, but at least I can make this room clean." This type of cleaning has a frantic, almost pathological quality to it. Sometimes I clean things twice, the object really being, not to make them clean, but to stay outside myself. Another defense of mine is exercise. A long run might be all it takes to nip the screams in the bud, and land me back in the realms of safety. It is rather hard to run and cry at the same time. If the pain is really bad and running has not helped then it is time for me to try to reach my doctor. In the past, he has prescribed a small quantity of a "rescue" medication for times such as these. Usually I did not need to take it — just knowing that it was there could get me through.

If my efforts to avoid the symptoms completely fail, then I know that I will have to tolerate them until they subside. There are activities that can help, even then. You may have been taught relaxation techniques in the hospital. These take practice, and can seem fairly pointless at first. If you do master them, they may at least reduce your stress, which will ease the intensity of your pain. I have found that doing things with my hands, such as sewing clothes by hand, can be extremely helpful, even when I am feeling really bad. I also find that painting or drawing can be soothing, although I am often frustrated by the results. Another helpful thing can be music, the types that help me most being "soft" rock, and really solid classical, such as Beethoven, played fairly loudly. For this, of course, you must have a music system, and understanding neighbors. I have also mentioned that when I feel bad, one way of fighting is to take care of my physical appearance. This helps me to feel less grotesque.

One more thing that I have found very helpful, is to own a pet. My dog has done wonders for me over the years. He can best be described as 80lb of love and saliva and not much else. We both enjoy his grooming, and we walk and run together. I must stress, however, that any animal is a responsibility, and needs room, time, and medical care. If you do not have sufficient funds or energy to care for and adequately train an animal, then to have one could be an expensive disaster. Bear in mind also, that many landlords do not allow pets, especially dogs, and that if you live in shared accommodation, you have to consider the effects that an animal could have on your room-mates. I have heard many consumers express how much their pets have benefited them, but do think carefully about the implications and expense of owning a pet, before making such a commitment.

One last general rule which seems to help, is to structure your time, especially when you are ill. Do not allow an unpunctuated day to stretch out before you. Have a routine that you follow even when it seems pointless. Make commitments to be with certain people at certain times. Set yourself deadlines — plan to accomplish a task by a definite time. You should not volunteer for so many activities that you subject yourself to stress, however, because this will only make your symptoms worse. But do keep busy.

Section 2. Monitor Yourself

The development of your arsenal, and its efficacy in helping you, depend entirely upon one thing — your ability to monitor your condition. I have not mentioned this before, because it is something that comes only with experience. At first you will need your doctor to monitor you, but you will learn to do this for yourself. You have to be a "seasoned campaigner" before you can recognize your own warning signs. Even now, my husband is sometimes the first to notice that I am not entirely well. The more ill I become, the less able I am to monitor myself. You also have to be honest with yourself, and realistic. This means that when you notice signs of impending trouble, you do not deny them. It is very tempting to do so, because the thought of more pain is naturally abhorrent to you. The trick is to recognize and acknowledge your warning signs and plan your strategy accordingly. There may even be physical signs that you can make use of. I have a characteristic rash that occurs when I am ill — sometimes I notice that before I notice the psychological warnings. As you become more familiar with the things your mind can do to you, you will find yourself thinking, "Hmm, I'm feeling angry / sad / anxious / etc, I wonder what that could be about?" If you can identify some event that might have precipitated an onset of your symptoms, you may be able to discuss this with someone, and so avert another episode of pain. The most important thing is to catch these things early, and <u>do something</u>, because, when left alone, they feed upon themselves, and weaken you. Even if you are not successful in your efforts to sidestep another episode, you will feel that you did at least try to help yourself, and you will have learned that that particular strategy was not successful for those circumstances. As I mentioned earlier, do not throw this weapon out completely, but file it away for the future when it may be useful to you, in different circumstances. I have noticed that even my fantasies can be a useful guide. If I find myself fantasizing about saving people's lives, usually by placing my own in jeopardy, then actually what I am doing is trying to compensate for a feeling of being worthless or inadequate. When I realize that, I can then start to "mobilize the troops".

Section 3. Unexpected Changes

The changes to which I am referring are those within yourself. By "unexpected", I do not mean "un-hoped-for" or undesirable, nor am I referring to those depths and sensitivities which you have acquired inevitably as a result of your experiences. The changes I want to discuss here are those that you are working toward in psychotherapy. The irony is that until they have happened, and manifest themselves in your behavior, you do not expect them ever to occur. Many people give up on therapy for a variety of reasons; however, most often the cause is that the consumer feels that, "It wasn't doing any good." Of course, there is a good chance that was true. The outcome of the therapeutic interaction depends entirely on the personalities involved and on the chemistry that exists between them. Sometimes it just does not work. The answer then, if funds allow, is to try another therapist, not to give up on therapy. Do not assume that, because one therapist could not help you, no one can. Let us suppose, however, that you do feel comfortable with your therapist, and that you usually come away from his or her office feeling a little better than when you walked in. You continue with therapy for that reason, but you may not feel that anything is really happening in the long term. Then, one day, some minor incident occurs and you find that you have reacted to it in a way that differs from the "normal" you. It is likely that you will not notice this as it occurs, but, having learned by now to monitor yourself, you look back and realize that you responded to the situation in a way that was new to you. It may be that you were more assertive than you used to be, or you were more able to control your aggression; you may find yourself unhurt by some comment that would formerly have devastated you. That is what I mean by "unexpected" changes. They are changes that allow you to cope better with the world in which you live, and they are what therapy is all about, but they happen with such subtlety that until they have already occurred you are not aware of them. You may not be aware of them even then. You may need your therapist, friend, or spouse to point out to you that your responses have changed.

There is, however, a drawback to the success of your therapy — your friends or family may not like these changes. Someone who is accustomed to bullying you may find that this is not so easy any more, and will of course object to the loss of power. Be prepared for people to tell you that your therapy is doing you no good, and that you should not continue with it. What they really mean, of course, is that your therapy is doing <u>them</u> no good because they can no longer manipulate you as they once could. This is hard to deal with, because it will have an effect on your relationships with these people and your new behaviors are not yet very well established. Try not to be deterred from continuing with your therapy, because the quality of your life is at stake. On the other hand, those who really are your allies will congratulate you, and will be genuinely pleased by your new-found strengths and coping mechanisms. Given the right therapist, and a willingness to contribute on your part, then therapy does work, but it does not happen overnight. If you persevere, and the outcome is good, then the effects are quite staggering. You will find yourself less afraid of a once hostile world, more able to trust yourself and your opinions, more able to interact effectively with others, and that being alive is more fun.

Lastly, you may find that you are more able to know and accept your limitations, without feeling that they are your fault. If you are only five feet tall then you are unlikely ever to be a huge success at probasketball. That is not your fault and it is unreasonable to blame yourself for it. Similarly, the limitations imposed on you by your illness are not your fault, and no one should ever hold you responsible for them. I have come to accept that when I am preoccupied by the screams that I hear, then I must not drive. To do so would be grossly irresponsible, because I am definitely impaired even though I have taken only my prescribed medication, and no other substances. I now do not undertake as many things as I once used to do, knowing that too much stress will bring back my symptoms, and I would then actually accomplish less than I do now.

Section 4. Contingency Plans

Speaking as one who has been hospitalized so many times, I can confidently say that returning to the hospital is strenuously to be avoided. If you start to find that your symptoms are becoming unmanageable once again, there should be a list of things that you can do to avoid the awful prospect of rehospitalization. Here are some suggestions, and you will, of course, formulate your own list to suit your needs. First tell your doctor, and discuss what might be going on in your life to make you feel overwhelmed. Discuss the possibility of more frequent sessions, or if this is unacceptable, stay in touch by phone. If you expect your doctor to call, do make sure the handset is properly placed, so that the line is free — some modern phones can be deceptive. Explore the possibility of a temporary modification in your medication, to get you through this rough patch. Try to get more rest, and pay attention to your diet. Make time for whatever exercise you find most relaxing. Remember — and I always have difficulty with this — that your problem is a medical one, it is a real illness and not your fault, much as some people would like to tell you otherwise. Therefore, if you are employed you must take sick-time if you need it. You would have to if you had the 'flu. As you know, I have found that sick-time taken for mental difficulties can cause problems, if your colleagues are not very enlightened. This is because they cannot see anything wrong with you, and your pain is not contagious. I am sure, however, that they would far rather have you missing for a week or so, than see you return to the hospital. If things really do get bad, then you might want to pack up your "psychiatric cosmetic-bag", and make arrangements for the welfare of any dependent relatives or animals that you normally care for. Remember, if you do have to go back into the hospital, it is not a failure on your part — an illness is an illness, and even with the best care, and all your hard work, it may still rear its ugly head once again. People with other types of illness have relapses, and sadly, this can also happen to you. I could never decide whether knowing roughly what to expect, after my first time in the hospital, was an advantage or not during the subsequent times. You do have the benefit of knowing that it will, at some point, end, but you also know about all the tedium and stupidity that you are going to have to put up with before you can, once again, control your own life.

The possibility of another stay in the hospital is a specter that will hang over your mind for some time after your first stay. It provides us all with a good incentive to take the medications, persevere with therapy, and formulate a good extensive arsenal of behaviors to reduce the likelihood of this unfortunate and disruptive outcome.

· 7 ·

Conclusion

If you have come this far with me, then I feel as though you are a dear friend, to whom I am sad to say farewell. I have, however, little else to offer you, ... but I would like to get up on my "soap-box" for a short while.

The problems of the mentally ill are horrendous. They have, if they are lucid enough to be aware of reality, three layers of pain. Primarily they have their symptoms. These take many different forms, from cleaning one's teeth with Lysol concentrate, to feeling responsible for the Mt. St. Helens disaster. All these symptoms, however, equate to pain on a grand scale, and should be treated with respect by us all. Secondarily, the mentally ill have to cope with the physical manifestations of their illness. By this I mean those problems that result directly from the primary pain and its treatment, for example, injuries caused by a suicide attempt, and/or the side-effects of a psychoactive medication. The tertiary pain, which the mentally ill have to cope with when they return to reality, comes from their awareness of the way in which society perceives them and their problems. In a word, stigma. This is improving, but we still have a long way to go. Recently, at the first meeting of a writing workshop, when asked to introduce myself, I mentioned my problems briefly, told them about this book, and voiced my desire to continue writing. The young man sitting next to me, himself a former patient, exclaimed in surprise at my "guts" in "confessing" to my problems. Why should it have to take guts to tell a roomful of strangers that you have a mental illness? Incidentally, it was not guts, rather defiance and my firm belief that stigma can only be overcome by our taking this sort of risk. I did not regret telling them — they were sensitive and gracious people. Nevertheless, this illustrates the problems faced, on a daily basis, by the less privileged mentally ill.

In Chapter Four I touched briefly upon my indignation at the use of psychiatric terminology out of its proper context. Why is it acceptable to label a piece of chocolate gateau, "Chocolate Suicide", when to label it a "Chocolate Carcinoma" would constitute almost criminal bad taste? The terms associated with schizophrenia are also bandied about most flippantly, even by educated people whose vocabularies must be large enough to provide them with alternatives. One young woman I know referred to her "schizophrenic" library. "Is her library really dislocated from reality?" I wondered. How about using "eclectic", or "diverse" instead? Only recently have I had the courage to challenge people over this, and the way I manage it, is by calmly and gently pointing out the actual meaning of these words, and asking the person whether that is what they really intended to say.

In Chapter Four I also touched upon the speculation that there may be a connection between madness and creativity. The question as to there being positive aspects to mental illness, was also mentioned. This fills me with unease. I will admit that the two references cited do show a correlation between affective disorders and creativity in writers. No such correlation was found in the case of schizophrenia. My question is, so what? Could it not simply be that a gene which confers potential creativity, happens to reside on the same chromosome as one which predisposes a person to affective disorder? If both of these were passed on to a child, then he or she might have a tendency toward both creativity and affective disorder. If, however only one of these genes were passed on, that would explain the existence of the many people who are creative, or have affective disorders, but not both.

I find very distasteful the suggestion that the mentally ill should redeem themselves by displaying "positive aspects." Does this mean that the most effective treatment could be withheld or refused by the patient, on the basis that it may destroy creativity? What does it say about us, as a society? Why can we not accept that the mentally ill are <u>ill</u>, and in <u>pain</u>, and respect them as such? Mental illness is hell, and the only "positive aspect" of it is that sometimes it goes away.

There may be a different type of connection between mental illness and creativity, however. As one reader of the New York Times recently suggested, artistic creativity may cause madness because of the poverty that tends to go with being an artist.[17] Alternatively, a person, disabled by mental pain, may start to explore his or her creative potential for solace, or money, or both, after regular employment is no longer possible. I am one of those.

Whatever the answers are to these questions, one thing is clear —
creative people who are mentally ill have more freedom to be
creative during a remission of their symptoms. How many more
wonderful sunflowers might there have been had Vincent Van Gogh
not killed himself?

Now I would like to address the problems that seem to exist
between the mental health professionals, and some of the mentally
ill. More than in other fields, a tension does exist between many
psychiatric consumers and those who care for them. Both approach
the other warily, the staff being ready for hostility and abuse, while
the consumer expects only tolerance, at best. This is not a simple
problem, as I have discovered. It becomes more complex, the longer
one thinks about it. I do not think that either "side" is at fault, or that
anyone wants to prolong this situation. I have found that this tension
can be rapidly dispelled if <u>both</u> parties are willing to reach across the
gap. One has to wonder, however, when both sides are striving for a
common goal, why there is a gap in the first place. I think the fault
lies, not in the patient or the staff member, but in the way mental
illness has been, and still is, perceived by our society.

Let us suppose that a perfectly ordinary family man starts
to hallucinate, have racing thoughts, and feelings of persecution. He
is frightened, and preoccupied, but because of the historical
associations that these problems have, he tells no one. His work
performance becomes erratic, he has difficulty keeping his
appointments, and his relationships with his family deteriorate. He
may even lose his job. His frantic wife, fearful for the survival of her
family, demands to know what is wrong. When he tells her, she is so
afraid that she rebukes him and tells him to "pull himself together".
So this person, through no fault of his own, has been rejected at both
his home, and his work, two of the most important aspects of his life.
These events serve only to confirm his suspicions of persecution.
Meanwhile his symptoms are worsening, due to stress and a lack of
needed treatment. He can still, with great effort, appear reasonably
"normal", so he starts to look for another job. The search is useless,
of course, because potential employers do not feel at ease with him:
they sense his confusion and have not received a good reference
from his former employer. At home, his behavior has become so
bizarre, that his wife is thinking of leaving him. A life is being

ruined, and these events will doubtless have their repercussions on the lives of his children, as they grow.

Now let us suppose that this man had become a diabetic. He would be very tired, lose weight, be very thirsty, and may even collapse during his weekly game of squash. Everyone, himself included, would realize that something was "legitimately" wrong, and they would seek help, because of their concern for him. He has a lifelong problem, but as everyone continues to believe in his validity as a person, the problem will be managed. With his psychiatric problem, by the time our hero actually meets a mental health professional, he has been rejected by so many once supportive people in his life, and his inner world has become so incomprehensible, that he may be defensive to the point of aggression.

Now let us consider the young mental health professional, full of energy and determined to help the mentally ill. She is a good listener, and readily makes herself available to his patients. Soon she is so swamped with grateful people, who have been rejected elsewhere — by their families, friends or by less caring staff — that she feels he has to defend herself to preserve her own sanity. So, she takes her home phone number out of the directory, and enlists the help of a secretary to answer her calls, thereby protecting herself from her patients. She also cultivates what is called "professional distance" behind which she is no less compassionate an individual, even though she seems so to those in her care. If, at the first encounter, either she or her patient feel that their worst expectations have been met, then the tension immediately increases. Of course, this can be said of any relationship, but in the field of psychiatry it is especially important. The therapeutic relationship must, to be effective, contain trust and respect on both sides. Therefore the suspicions that exist between consumers and professionals are particularly obstructive to good treatment.

This is not the whole story, however. There is also the issue of restraint. To ignore the fact that people with mental illness are sometimes violent, would be to undermine the fabric of this text. During the worst period of my illness, I needed to be restrained for my own safety, even though I am one of those souls who rescue birds and spiders and earthworms, to return them to their natural environment. The symptoms of these horrible diseases render the consumer susceptible to the most incomprehensible pain and frustration. It is a fact that most violence committed by consumers is directed against themselves, usually in an attempt to end the pain, or at least to make it tangible. This does not make restraint any less necessary, but because of the connotations that being "locked up" carry, it is definitely a source of stress between consumers and staff. Someone who is in a state of "diminished responsibility", due to his or her illness, is nevertheless, <u>still a person</u>, deserving of sympathy and respect. Already, the need for, and use of, restraint on psychiatric wards, is much reduced, due to the greater efficacy of the medications that we now have available.

It would be both stupid and insulting to pretend that either the consumers, or the professionals are all angels. Both are simply cross-sections of humanity, one suffering from illness, and the other trying to do a job. However, the way our society perceives and treats the mentally ill, colors the way that they interact with each other, so that a truly therapeutic relationship is harder to establish. This not only prolongs the victim's pain, but is also more costly; to the consumer, to the insurance company, and/or to the government. Somehow we must break this silly impasse.

I hope and believe that the answer lies in solid scientific knowledge about the vast array of ailments that are currently known as "mental illness". History is cluttered with examples of illnesses which were then seen as a product of the patient's imagination. They therefore were not treated with respect, until a tangible cause for them, such as the tuberculosis bacillus, was found. I believe that is where we are now, with mental illness. Researchers are only just starting to unearth the biochemical realities of these ailments. One young psychiatrist I know, when hearing the type of brain scan that he works with described as "a window" on the brain, remarked to me, "It's actually a pin-hole." He was trying to illustrate how very little is known, and how far there is to go, before we will master this field. Diagnoses are made on the basis of the consumer's behavior and on anecdotal evidence alone. As there are no definitive laboratory tests for any particular mental illness, these awful problems are not really seen as legitimate by many people. There are real and quantifiable differences, however, between the brains of people with mental illnesses, as compared to those without such problems.[18] When there are routine diagnostic tests for the various mental illnesses — and I say "when" because I firmly believe this will happen — then perhaps we can give these problems specific names, and bring them into the realms of legitimate illness, where they have always belonged. Until then, it is a sad fact that to have a mental illness renders one suspect. Now I must confess to the most stupid aspect of myself. When I am really ill, even I do not believe in the validity of my pain. I have an M.Sc. in biochemistry, and am married to a chemist who works in diagnostic psychiatry, and even I cannot at times believe that I am really ill. I besiege my poor doctor with questions as to whether I am "making it up". Such is the power of societal conditioning.

I wish that one day, all forms of mental illness will be readily accepted in our society; stand-up comics will no longer gain mileage from tales of how only depressed and schizophrenic dolphins get caught in tuna-nets, and mentioning your bout of depression to your boss will no longer be a matter for debate. I hope most fervently that one day, someone will wonder why it was ever thought necessary to write this book.

Appendix: Your Legal Rights.

Although it may not seem so now, you do have legal rights, and you should know how to find out about them. As far as I know, there is, in every hospital, a "Patient's Advocate" or "Ombudsperson" who can explain your legal status to you. Basically, the issues usually revolve around those of restraint. In the legislatures that I studied, I found that there are several layers of potential force which can be used to keep you in the hospital. By "force" I mean legal mechanisms, not chains! Obviously, the most desirable situation is that you are well enough to recognize your need for help and that you enter the hospital as a "voluntary patient". This may also be referred to as an "informal admission". This means that you can choose to leave the hospital against medical advice, and, unless they can prove that you are a danger to yourself or others, they are not permitted to detain you. If, however, they can prove that your are in danger, the staff can detain you for a short period — usually, 72 hours — during which time they will discuss with you the implications of your leaving and whether you can handle being "outside". If you can convince them that you will be safe, they may discharge you before your 72 hours are up, or you can decide to stay on as a voluntary patient. If, after the 72 hours, they are still concerned for your safety, then there is usually a mechanism by which they can detain you for a longer period, and you are then an involuntary patient. Your doctor <u>must</u> have documented proof to justify this action, and you have the right to see this, and your clinical records. During this time you will be given treatment just like any other patient. At the end of that time, you will either be well enough to leave, or you may stay on as a voluntary patient until you are well. On the other hand, if you are still considered to be at risk at the end of this time, the staff can detain you, against your will, for an even longer period, usually three to six months. If you reach this level of detention, you will know far more about the legislature in your particular state or province, than I can tell you.

The main point is that at each level of detention, the staff must be able to prove that their actions are justified. Also, remember that you have a right to ask for your clinical record and for communication with anyone. Occasionally these requests may be refused by the staff, on the grounds that they may be detrimental to your state of mind or your social status. This means that, for example, if you were delusional, or very disturbed, the nature of what you might communicate could lead to trouble for you after your recovery. As with detention, the staff must be able to prove that these actions were justified.

It is very important for your peace of mind that these things are made clear to you by the staff. If you do not understand what is happening to you, you can ask for the patient advocate to explain it, either to you, or to someone you trust. Remember, the very fact that you are ill may make you feel confused, and your medication will probably contribute to that. So, you may feel that the staff are hiding things from you, even when they are actually doing their best to help you. They do not want to detain you any longer than is necessary — they want to get you well, and out in the world so that they can get on with the next job. It seems to me, these days, that most problems arise from premature discharge, rather than overlong detention, so it is unlikely that you will ever have to deal with these issues.

Bibliography

1. Styron W. (1990). Darkness Visible. A Memoir of Madness. Random House of Canada Ltd, New York/Toronto,.
2. Guze S.B. and Robins E. (1970) Suicide and Primary Affective Disorders. Brit. J. Psychiatry, 117: 437-438.
3. Salzman B. (1996). The Handbook of Psychiatric Drugs. Henry Holt & Co, New York,.
4. Opler L.A. (1996). Prozac and Other Psychiatric Drugs. Everything You Need to Know. Simon & Schuster, New York,.
5. Levitt A.J. (1992) The Management of Seasonal Affective Disorder. Contemporary Psychiatry, Aug/Sept: 9-17.
6. Levitt A.J., et al. (1993) Side Effects of Light Therapy in Seasonal Affective Disorder. Am. J. Psychiatry, 150: 650-652.
7. Maxman J.S. (1986) Essential Psychopathology. Penguin Books Canada Ltd. Markham Ont. p198.
8. Konnor M. (1987) Becoming a Doctor. A Journey of Initiation in Medical School. Haddon Craftsmen. Scranton Pa. p170.
9. Greben S.E., et al. (1985) A Method of Psychiatry. Lea & Febiger. Philadelphia. p 361. -
10. Greben S.E., et al. (1985) A Method of Psychiatry. Lea & Febiger, Philadelphia. p206.
11. Murray R. and Huelskoetter M.M.W. (1983) Psychiatric/Mental Health Nursing. Giving Emotional Care. Prentice-Hall Inc. Englewood Cliffs. p34.
12. Vonnigut M. (1975). The Eden Express. Preager Publishers Ltd, New York,.
13. Wessely S. (1993) The Times (London), 13 July: p15.
14. Andreasen N.C. (1987) Creativity and Mental Illness: Prevalence in Writers and Their First-Degree Relatives. Am. J. Psychiatry, 144: 1288-1292.
15. Andreasen N.C. and Canter A. (1974) The Creative Writer: Psychiatric Symptoms and Family History. Comprehensive Psychiatry, 15: 123-131.

16. Community Resources Consultants of Toronto (1997) Making Choices: A Consumer/Survivors' Guide to Adult Mental Health Services in Metro Toronto. (Free to consumers in Toronto Area). Community Resource Consultants of Toronto. Toronto.
17. Meyers B. (1993) Don't Leap to Conclusions About Genius. The New York Times, Oct 18:
18. Seeman P., et al. (1993) Dopamine D4 Receptors Elevated in Schizophrenia. Nature, 365: 441-444.

ISBN 1-55212-213-1